ADVANCE PRAISE FOR *LEADING CHANGE*

"*Leading Change* humanizes and simplifies the change management process. Dan Mann leverages a wide variety of relatable examples, along with his extensive experience, to entertain and inspire me to be a better leader. The variety of examples from the sports, business, and music worlds make this book a highly relatable and interesting read, with a simple-to-follow roadmap to help leaders solve complex problems."

—**NOLAN MOSER**, assistant vice president, Shimano Bicycle

"Dan Mann's approach to turning a vision into reality is spot-on. His Gentle Pressure Relentlessly Applied methodology puts the basic blocking and tackling of leadership into terms that leaders in all stages of their careers can easily understand and apply. These solid leadership principles have stood the test of time. I will be ordering a copy of this book for my entire leadership team, at every level of the organization."

—**TODD OUELLETTE**, owner and president, Long-Lewis Auto Group, and finalist, TIME Dealer of the Year

"In *Leading Change*, Dan Mann has created a map for making change that is highly effective yet remarkably simple to follow. Dan is a gifted coach who is a master at applying gentle persuasion to achieve transformational change. This book is well-researched, equal parts strategic and simple, and contains powerful lessons for today's leaders. Highly recommend."

—BLAIR CLARK, president, Canyon US

"*Leading Change* is a beautifully written and effective follow-up to Dan Mann's first book, *ORBiT*. It details a common-sense roadmap for success and reminds us that there are no shortcuts for a leader looking to establish a culture of accountability in their organization. There is, however, a highly effective structure and process for bringing about such change. In *Leading Change*, Mann shows us the way."

—KELLY KNIGHT, Sun & Ski Sports

"Organizational change is never easy, and at times it can be downright scary. Working closely with Dan Mann, Red Rock Running Company was able to enact organizational change which made us an industry leader, setting standards in many key metrics that make us the envy of our peers. If you are looking for the leader's secret weapon to lasting change, this is the book for you."

—MARK JIMENEZ, EdD, owner, Red Rock Running Company

"Dan Mann's *Leading Change* is the perfect combination of philosophy and application that leaders need to succeed in business today. Mann combines his expertise, honed through years of practical application, with his storytelling skills to give us implementation examples that are spot-on and easy to apply. His Gentle Pressure Relentlessly Applied framework is powerful and comprehensive yet simple, with tools and applications that are repeatable and proven, along with a comprehensive process anyone can follow."

—**TODD DAULHAUSER**, global brand president, Dickies, and VF Corporation executive team

"Too many books about enacting change are full of theory and high-level ideas which leave you asking, 'What do I actually do with this?' Dan Mann's *Leading Change* and his Gentle Pressure Relentlessly Applied framework come from the experience and perspective of an actual practitioner. The framework leaps off the page with real-in-market examples, and the book will leave you superbly prepared to lead change in your own organization."

—**RYAN MCCARTY**, founder, Collective 12

LEADING CHANGE

LEADING CHANGE

HOW TO ACHIEVE SUPERIOR RESULTS WITH GENTLE PRESSURE RELENTLESSLY APPLIED

DAN MANN

Leading Change:
How to Achieve Superior Results with Gentle Pressure Relentlessly Applied
Copyright © 2023, Dan Mann

All rights reserved. No part of this publication may be reproduced or transmitted in any form or by any means, mechanical or electronic, including photocopying and recording, or by any information storage or retrieval system, without permission in writing from author (except by a reviewer, who may quote brief passages and/or show brief video clips in a review).

Disclaimer: The advice and strategies contained herein may not be suitable for your situation and should not replace the advice of a professional. The author shall not be liable for damages arising herefrom.

ISBN (paperback): 979-8-9879045-0-3
ISBN (hardcover): 979-8-9879045-1-0
ISBN (e-book): 979-8-9879045-2-7
ISBN (audiobook): 979-8-9879045-3-4
Library of Congress Control Number: 2023903598

Edited by Jocelyn Carbonara
Proofread by Amy Weinstein
Interior and cover design by George Stevens

Published by The Mann Group, Weaverville, NC, USA

For Leslie, who chooses me every day,
even though she doesn't have to.

CONTENTS

Preface..xiii

Introduction...1

PART ONE 11
EXPLORING THE CONCEPTS

Chapter 1	Change Leaders from John Kennedy to Luke Skywalker..13
Chapter 2	Gentle Pressure Relentlessly Applied—A Mantra and a Process................................. 23

PART TWO 51
FROM CONCEPT TO APPLICATION

Chapter 3	A Closer Look at the Infographic 53
Chapter 4	"If Running Is Difficult, Run More"—Focusing on Your Outcomes..................................61
Chapter 5	Agreement on Approach 81
Chapter 6	Metrics for Assurance......................... 113
Chapter 7	Training and Coaching.........................129
Chapter 8	Implementing Phase Four—Culture of Accountability.................................153

Conclusion 183

Acknowledgments... 189

Connect with The Mann Group.............................. 193

Also by Dan Mann 197

References 199

About the Author 203

PREFACE

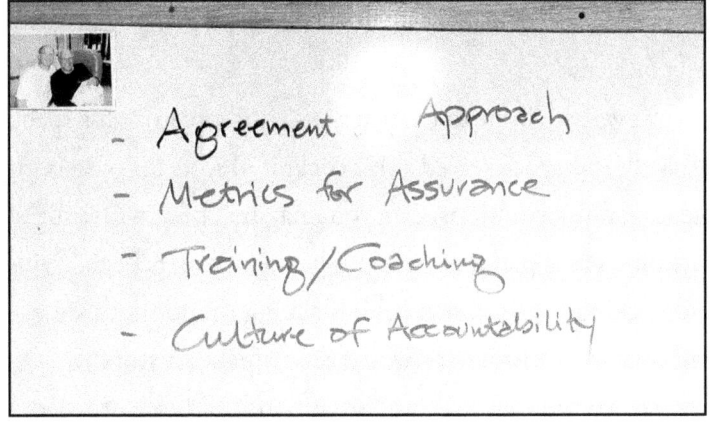

RESULTS AREN'T GUARANTEED, even on the most robust teams with the strongest leaders.

As my partner, Leslie, and I gathered in the office of Derek Stepanek, the fourth-generation owner of Northtowne Cycling and Fitness in Cedar Rapids, Iowa, we could see the frustration etched onto his face. He'd asked us to help develop his 2019 strategy, which involved assessing his management structure, since his desired results eluded him.

Our company, the Mann Group, often gets called due to a disconnect between current metrics and desired results. Our job is to close that gap. It isn't always quite that simple, but you might be surprised that it's also not that complicated.

Years of doing everything himself had meant that Derek's office had become a de facto filing system for every note, business card, receipt, and special order that had been acquired under his watch. As we gazed around his office, we could see that he knew where everything was—but only *he* knew.

So we set about to change that—and organize his space. After all, this space served as his cockpit of sorts for overseeing the rest of his operations. Can you imagine a pilot with a messy cockpit? As the plane ascends, his personal papers begin flying and sticking to the windshield, blocking the copilot's view—and the rest is history (or worse yet, it makes history!).

So we purged. We organized. And he began to sweat. But slowly, progress occurred—not just on his office, but in his mind. Leslie and I talked him through why and how he needed to change (no—*transform!*) not only his office space, but his very approach to management.

But *how* would he change?

He would *invest in others*. He would *build process*. He would *create accountability*.

"Derek," I kept saying throughout our intervention, "You have to live by the mantra, Gentle Pressure Relentlessly Applied."

Out of frustration, Derek finally said, "Dan, I've heard you use that phrase many times before. But I don't know what it means or how to apply it to the situation I'm in right now!"

Putting aside the stacks of notebooks and extra office equipment piled around me, I erased the office whiteboard. Next, I wrote four statements on it:

1. Agreement on Approach
2. Metrics for Assurance
3. Training/Coaching
4. Culture of Accountability

As I wrote, I explained each concept. Derek listened, absorbed, nodded, and asked questions.

After a one-hour session, Leslie looked at the board, locked eyes back on me, and smiled. "There it is," she said, her eyes clearly excited.

"There's what?" I asked, confused.

She looked at me with that Leslie-knows-something-you-don't-know smile.

"There's your next book!"

We visited Derek's store a year later, and our words remained on his white board.

Derek, this book exists in your honor—because of your hard work to transform your behaviors and bring about a Culture of Accountability in your company.

And it exists for all of you who are about to do the same.

INTRODUCTION

ON APRIL 17, 2018, Southwest Airlines Flight 1380 departed from New York for Dallas, Texas. What had been a routine flight was dramatically interrupted by the terrifying sounds of engine and fuselage failure. Engine debris flew through the air and damaged a window, partially sucking a passenger outside the aircraft.

In the midst of tragedy, triumph showed up. The quick reflexes of the pilot, Tammie Jo Shults—coupled with her years of Navy training—saved all but one passenger that day. A transcript of the pilot calling for help shows a calm, trained voice—impressively navigating the aircraft and its occupants to safety.

Those in near-miss situations like this often report what happens during that gap between when danger hits, and when the all-clear sounds. In many cases, passengers and crew report recalibrating to what matters most to them, as they face their potential loss of life. Doreen Welsh, flight attendant on the famed "Miracle on the Hudson" US Airways Flight 1549, speaks publicly about what she learned about her life in the ninety seconds between hearing the dreaded words, "Brace for impact," and hitting the water. "If you only had ninety seconds to make an impact, what would you do?" she asks her audiences. And she speaks about how her crew kicked into action once they heard those words—applying what they had repeatedly practiced in drills. Because they had trained for such contingencies, they managed to get everyone off the plane alive—and relatively well (Welsh 2010).

Not everyone practices for tragedy, however. So what happens when it finds those of us who are untrained for its effects?

As the Southwest Airlines Flight 1380 crew responded with practiced emergency protocol after the failure of one engine and subsequent tragedy with the passenger partially out the window, the other passengers did exactly what you or I would do in the same situation. They attempted to reach their loved ones on the ground. They held hands with family, friends, and even strangers. They prayed. And of course, they put on those yellow oxygen masks, deployed from overhead to prevent the effects of hypoxia: numbness, nausea, and eventually, loss of consciousness.

In our twenty-four-hour news cycle, the media was quick to publish the first pictures from inside the cabin. One passenger, Marty Martinez, posted a selfie, which showed dozens of rows of passengers behind and beside him.

Perusing the photos, once you got past the fear and anxiety clearly displayed on these faces, you'd notice something else: everyone was wearing their oxygen masks *incorrectly*! They had the masks over only their mouths—not their noses. This could easily have resulted in a reduction of oxygen to the brain and the resulting dangerous symptoms of hypoxia; but that detail about losing life and limb to an improperly donned mask was apparently lost in the hubbub of tragedy on board.

If you've ever flown on a commercial flight, you've seen (or at least *heard*, as you distracted yourself with last-minute texts to colleagues or family) the safety demonstrations. "Place the mask over your mouth and nose, like this. Pull the strap to tighten it. If you are traveling with children, make sure that your own mask is on first before helping your children." Sound familiar?

The airlines have various methods to communicate this procedure to passengers. They show onboard videos, some of which include clever attention-grabbing details. Their flight attendants actually conduct a demonstration, showing how it's done. And each seat pocket includes a laminated drawing with written instructions. You could say that the airline industry has used "Gentle Pressure Relentlessly Applied" (which we will explain in a bit) in an attempt to mitigate risk and ensure safety. Or have they? Let's explore.

On April 17, 2018, their mask trainings didn't work. But why not? After all, surely the airline safety folks put their best communications experts on the job of creating messaging, right?

I'll give you several possibilities why that wasn't enough to ensure compliance—and an outcome of oxygen safety. Perhaps:

- The passengers never felt that this procedure would be needed, so they never paid attention.
- One passenger put the mask on incorrectly, and others followed suit—believing that was how it should be done.
- They were under trauma, in a rush, and not thinking clearly.
- They'd never had the opportunity to actually practice with an oxygen mask prior to the emergency.
- The oxygen masks were designed poorly, and their use wasn't intuitive.

If you are in the business of leading change, you likely understand how this situation could happen. In times of change—especially when emotions are high—it's not enough to assume people know what to do. Planning and intentional processes must be put into place to circumvent all possible scenarios where people fail to comply with the most important protocols. But how?

Let's start by examining this seemingly innocent breakdown on the Southwest flight, because in fact, it mimics a common breakdown that occurs during change. Fortunately, there's also a common process we can apply to mitigate any poor outcome—and ensure success in your change initiative.

The process of Gentle Pressure Relentlessly Applied isn't just an accidental approach to creating change. It must be intentional. It must be specific. Ultimately it must work—or it won't be an effective leadership tool.

So, let's look at the failure in this process on board Southwest:

1. **Was there an *Agreement* from all passengers on the approach to using the masks?** In other words, did the flight crew ensure that everyone on board understood what was required of them and showed willingness to participate? Did they all agree that the airline's process was the right approach? Did the airline confirm this with everyone?
2. **Was there some *Metric for Assurance*?** Was there a visible way to measure the effort, so that each passenger could confirm, without doubt, that they had installed the mask correctly? (Think of all the metrics associated with deep sea diving and the risks of using that equipment incorrectly!) Could the flight crew confirm the proper implementation of the masks via some measurement that was readily available to them? (Consider the verbal "yes" required by those sitting in an emergency exit row when asked by the flight attendant if they are able and willing to assist in the case of emergency. A passenger's response serves as a preliminary metric to measure probable compliance.)
3. **Was there effective *Training and Coaching?*** During the actual deployment of the masks, was there some opportunity for in-the-moment coaching? Did all

passengers want the training? Did everyone know what was at stake?

4. **Was there some sort of *Culture of Accountability* associated with everyone's responsibility in this type of event—such as follow-up to ensure compliance?** Was anyone charged with guaranteeing the successful, accurate deployment of this safety feature?

The answer to each of these questions—with the exception of the one addressing training—is a resounding *no*. When you look at the events of Southwest Flight 1380 in this context, you can thus quickly see there would have been a better way.

Each of these questions explores the four main phases of Gentle Pressure Relentlessly Applied process:

1. Agreement on Approach
2. Metrics for Assurance
3. Training and Coaching
4. Culture of Accountability

As you read and discover more about the process I will outline in this book, you'll begin to apply these phases (in retrospect) to the situations you've been responsible for that didn't turn out like you planned—particularly around change. You'll quickly diagnose why your expectations weren't realized. You'll view your unintended consequences in a new light. You'll think, *I can see now why that happened*. In some cases, you may even come to an inevitable conclusion: *that had no chance of succeeding!*

Ah, the beauty of hindsight.

So, choose right now to be effective in your future change initiatives. Choose to learn from these errors and go forward into the future with a better plan. Arm yourself with these new tools—and a new process—to ensure your success with your team.

Ultimately, if you want to change something, and you are in charge—formally or informally—*you* will be *leading change*. I've used the phrase Gentle Pressure Relentlessly Applied since the early nineties when I first heard it (which I will explain more later). But this idiom is more than a motivational poster slogan. This concept actually can be implemented with intent, consistency, measurable results, and confidence.

And you don't need to limit yourself to using the Gentle Pressure Relentlessly Applied process only at work—although the emphasis of this book will be on the workplace. The Gentle Pressure Relentlessly Applied process exists as a failure analysis for every change effort you attempted but didn't achieve. This may include:

- That promotion to regional VP you took, subsequently washing out after the first year as you failed to achieve its job expectations;
- That company you started with the intent to "change the world," but after failing to build the right team, it never came to fruition;
- That soccer team you coached through the pre-season with such high hopes, only to end with a 1–18 record; or

- That situation you're in now—with no progress, no results, and no idea what to do about it.

Gentle Pressure Relentlessly Applied also exists to give you hope that:

- There is a proven formula for achieving success with a team;
- There is a way to achieve those ever-elusive results you're after; and
- If you choose the narrow path of leadership, it can (and will) pay off.

As we explore this approach in detail throughout this book, think about how you will apply it while:

- Leading a sales team
- Raising children
- Building a business
- Coaching fifth-grade soccer
- Transforming a toxic culture

You don't necessarily need a formal leadership role or title to apply these principles. You can find value in the principles wherever you fall on the organizational chart, although those with leadership responsibilities will find them most crucial.

One thing is certain: Gentle Pressure Relentlessly Applied isn't static. These four words, taken together, indicate active intent. There are no wasted words. Each one builds on the one before it, representing an important theme in the process, and together they communicate your intent to lead change.

So let's get started: what do you want to change?

PART ONE
EXPLORING THE CONCEPTS

CHAPTER 1

CHANGE LEADERS FROM JOHN KENNEDY TO LUKE SKYWALKER

CHANGE IS A simple word, with a complexity of meaning:

- To make different
- To transform
- To replace one with another

You can change your mind, change your address, change your clothes, change your hair color, change your schedule, or change your life. There's certainly no shortage of self-help books offering a pathway to life changes.

Change happens to us almost daily—as we adjust to weather, traffic, illness. Those are the changes we often perceive as negative, and we must find our way around them. But change can also be positive—like giving birth to a child, getting a new job, or moving employees to a brand-new building.

Change typically falls within two categories. It occurs as a result of:

1. A realized *obstacle*, or
2. A perceived *opportunity*.

If you are a manager or leader, you're likely charged with the task of improving or maintaining a process, service, experience, product, or the like. Human nature being what it is, you're facing the likelihood that you must change your team's behavior in order to accomplish the task. Spoiler alert: this means you *are* a change manager, even if your job title doesn't mention it.

Next, we will explore the two types of change.

OBSTACLES THAT CALL FOR CHANGE

Let's say you manage a medical center where the standards of cleanliness are stringently prescribed and must be met each hour of the day. However, some of your staff are focused on their lunch schedules and their need to leave work exactly at 5:00 p.m. Additionally, the cleaning tasks are difficult and require the use of gloves and harsh chemicals. Your team doesn't want to participate, and since you're responsible for the outcome, you find yourself doing all the cleaning. *You need to create change around an obstacle.*

On a personal level, an obstacle might be that you experience a health scare. Your heart is fluttering out of control, and while you learn that the arrhythmia is benign, you discover in the process that your blood pressure is sky-high. You could take medication, but your doctor says you can first try lifestyle changes to improve your numbers. You decide to change how you eat and move each day. *Again, you're creating change around an obstacle.*

OPPORTUNITIES THAT CALL FOR CHANGE

You've just been promoted to manager of an underperforming pizza restaurant in your town. This restaurant is one of twenty-five in a regional chain. The store underperforms because of inconsistent food quality, subpar restaurant cleanliness, and ineffective marketing. Then you're offered a bonus structure that pays you 5 percent of all profits once the restaurant hits its annual revenue goals. You see a financial and career opportunity here, but *you need to create change to lean into an opportunity.*

On the personal side, let's say you are out to dinner with friends, when one of them says, "Hey, I just signed up for a half marathon in the fall. You should join me!" Before you can take another bite, you chime in, "Sure!" Then when you get home that night, you ask yourself, *What was I thinking? I haven't run a mile since grade school!* You begin Googling "couch to 5k" programs, and you decide to *change your fitness level to achieve this opportunity.*

If a change is strictly personal, you can likely engage in it without much cooperation from others. But in the case of the workplace (or any change involving others), you—the manager—must work through others to achieve change.

As a change manager, it's helpful to know that most people—unless they consciously decide or are forced to think otherwise—will settle into a routine existence that they never leave. This is because people generally experience stress around the idea of change, even when it's positive. They may want to change, but their minds are conditioned to stay with what they know. Even the most anticipated changes require adjustment. Just think of all of the adjustment when a new baby is brought home! Stress is embedded into even the most positive changes, and humans tend to resist stress.

You as a manager aren't immune to that human resistance. So keep that in mind as you work through the Gentle Pressure Relentlessly Applied process.

Once you fully support a change, it can be maddening to attempt to create the behaviors you want in others. This is what separates great coaches and teachers from average ones. So what makes the difference?

I find that leaders who are successful in guiding others through change have uncovered the *reason why* someone would want to change. After all, why would I want to work harder? Why would I want to sacrifice? Why would I want to give up my comfort? Change engagement requires a meaningful reason why, so that others can see "what's in it for me?" (often abbreviated to WIFM).

Consider these powerful examples of effective "whys" around change:

- Luke Skywalker changed his mind about going to Alderaan with Obi-Wan Kenobi, because his remaining family was killed and he wanted revenge (Star Wars).
- Rocky Balboa suddenly got serious about his training once he realized this was his opportunity to show he was "not just some bum from the neighborhood" (Rocky).
- John McClane went from being a run-of-the-mill New York cop to virtual superhero once his wife, Holly, was captured by terrorists (Die Hard).
- Po went from fat and lazy to Kung Fu warrior once he realized that his friends were in trouble and the Dragon Scroll was nothing but a mirror (Kung Fu Panda).

While these fictional stories illustrate the point, real-life examples are usually less dramatic. Yet effective leaders also make the effort to identify those "reasons why" people would work hard, change their habits, grow new skills, and make sacrifices. Consider these leadership examples:

- John Kennedy: "I believe that this nation should commit itself to achieving the goal, before this decade is out, of landing a man on the moon and returning him safely to Earth."
- Martin Luther King, Jr.: "I have a dream that my four little children will one day live in a nation where they will not be judged by the color of their skin but by the content of their character."

And more recently, consider the following mission statements.

- Microsoft: "A computer on every desk and in every home."
- Disney: "To entertain, inform, and inspire people through the power of unparalleled storytelling."
- Southwest Airlines: "To become the world's most loved, most efficient, and most profitable airline."

In each of these examples, a leader—or leadership team—was able to clearly define that which was worth changing for. They *put it out there* and committed to it. People could see what was in it for them, and they wanted to be a part of the change.

While their purpose may have been stated simply, it was powerful and compelling.

In fact, it may actually have been scary too! Imagine how the audience might have felt in 1961 as John Kennedy effectively said, "We should go to the moon!" Yet his vision—his *reason why*—created a coalition of unlikely partners. Politicians, scientists, the military, *Life Magazine*, engineers, educators, and hundreds of others began to work harder, make changes, sacrifice, and bring something new into existence. They all became fully invested in the change—because they understood why it was happening.

This all happened because someone saw an opportunity, communicated it, and inspired others into action. At some level, you must do the same thing in order to effectively lead change.

A LIFE-ALTERING NEED FOR CHANGE

We've explored some fictional changes—and sweeping changes initiated by legendary leaders. Now, let's explore a more "everyday" management change which involved yours truly.

In April 1992, I was promoted to my first management position for Bachrach, a men's clothing company. I became the store manager at the Hickory Ridge Mall in Memphis, Tennessee. At the time, I didn't know what I was facing. In the previous year, Hickory Ridge was the lowest volume store in the Bachrach organization. Worse, it had an inventory shrink (loss) of an astounding 16 percent. This was not a good store.

I walked in on my first day—proud and optimistic—and saw immediately why the store performed so poorly:

- The staff wasn't wearing the company dress code (we sold men's suits and accessories, so this mattered!).
- The back storage room was dirty, messy, and disorganized.
- The sales floor was poorly displayed, with sloppy product merchandising.

I went to work. Without any management training at the time, I relied on my instinct.

First, I felt I needed to set a new example. So for my first three days, I took off my jacket and fully cleaned and organized the back room—and established new rules for what employees could and couldn't do back there.

Next, I pulled my team together, and we re-merchandised the store. New displays. Crisp folds. Vacuumed, Windexed, and restocked throughout.

I also called early meetings and offered sales training. I was on my way to turning things around! The results showed.

But then, I discovered something startling. During a routine audit of some product returns, I found some internal theft. With my heart in my throat, I called our company loss prevention director, Randy Council. To my further surprise, he already knew. And he was relieved that I had discovered the issue and reported it. As it turned out, the internal theft was widespread in my store.

Randy and I met in person at a local restaurant, and he delivered the bad news: there were only two honest people working in the store—my assistant manager and me. Randy then informed me of what I already knew: company policy required that we fire and prosecute every one of the dishonest employees.

But he left it to me to decide whether or not to take action.

"Dan, I know that if we do this, your assistant might quit too, and then you'll have no one," he added. "I'm sorry. I'll give you the option. Because of the extreme nature of this situation, I can give you some time to prep, so it won't be so bad for you."

This was one of the most challenging experiences of my career. But I was clear about what I needed to do. I wouldn't work in a situation where my team was working against me. I hadn't hired many of these folks, and it was clear they weren't on board with my new way. I felt that I would rather do this by myself than work with dishonest people. I knew I could do what was needed next.

"Randy, let's do it today," I said. "I'll call them into the store, and you and your team can take them out."

I called them in, and he removed them one by one. I experienced what happens as a result of sloppy leadership, no accountability, and a lack of culture. This was an important moment for my management career. No one wants to have to go through a mass firing, but in this case, it was necessary in order to initiate the changes that the store needed. And I never wanted to go through anything like it again while working there, which meant I would need to build a better team from the ground up.

I went to my application file, set interview appointments, made urgent phone calls, and networked in the business community. Within three days, I had hired and trained the new team, and we set a course for a better store and improved results. This change initiative became a career choice that has paid personal dividends for me for decades. I became a change leader in that role, even though I didn't realize it at the time.

And I'm guessing you are a change leader too. What's your situation?

- Do you experience a constant flow of distractions and disputes from your team?
- Are you doing all the work while others sit by and watch?

- Do you have team members who "have great potential" but just can't seem to break through with consistent performance and results?
- Are you wondering if it's really worth it to be in a leadership position?
- Are your results not clearly reflective of your effort?
- Or are you formally leading a change initiative—such as an enterprise resource planning (ERP) conversion, merger, or leadership transition?

Now that we've established that you are in the business of change, we'll explore the Gentle Pressure Relentlessly Applied process. Keep reading!

CHAPTER 2

GENTLE PRESSURE RELENTLESSLY APPLIED—A MANTRA AND A PROCESS

THE FIRST TIME I can remember hearing the phrase Gentle Pressure Relentlessly Applied was in the fall of 1993. I was in Decatur, Illinois, at a management workshop being led by a company. The phrase instantly resonated with me, and I began using it regularly as a manager. At The Mann Group, we now use the phrase almost weekly in our Mann University program (it's actually pre-printed on our name tents!).

As I've conducted research for this book, I've become increasingly interested in finding the original author. I've found several recent uses of the phrase across the internet, including some similar sounding phrases like, "constant gentle pressure," which is used by restauranteur Danny Meyer of the Union Square Hospitality Group.

I found a source which indicated the phrase was first used by Ray Eliot, former coach of the University of Illinois football team (1942–1959). He developed some notoriety for an inspiring speech titled, "The Proper State of Mind." My resource indicated that he used the phrase in this speech. After a Google search, I found the speech, listened to it multiple times, but didn't hear Coach Eliot mention "Gentle Pressure Relentlessly Applied."

I exhausted all my resources, only to determine that there are likely many authors to the phrase (Edwards and Wintle 2013). I use it frequently and appreciate it—but I certainly didn't originate it. As of today, the original source is still a mystery to me.

What I intend to do in this chapter is to explain this phrase to you, and then throughout this book, I will make it as practical and implementable as possible in the context of change management. The concept is easy to understand. The application requires focus, work, determination, and planning. The payoff? Improved results.

In this chapter, we also will explain what each *theme* word—*gentle, pressure, relentlessly,* and *applied*—means in the context of the Gentle Pressure Relentlessly Applied *process*.

ADOPTING THE PROPER STATE OF MIND

"Thinking"

If you think you're beaten, you are;
If you think you dare not, you don't.

> If you'd like to win, but think you can't,
> It's almost a cinch that you won't.
> If you think you'll lose, you've lost;
> For out in this world we find
> Success begins with a fellow's will.
> It's all in the state of mind.
> If you think you're outclassed, you are;
> You've got to think high to rise.
> You've got to be sure of yourself before
> You can ever win the prize.
> Life's battles don't always go
> To the stronger or faster man;
> But sooner or later the person who wins
> Is the one who thinks he can!
> —*Walter Wintle, poet (1905)*

This poem was referenced in Ray Eliot's speech, with Eliot's own adaptations and interpretations made. He ended it by saying: "It's all a state of mind." Ray Eliot was a successful college football coach and a skilled speaker. You can see in some of the old-school language (suggesting that it's all about men, fellows, battles, and success) in this poem he quoted that Coach Eliot's paradigm was the football field. Don't miss the fact, though, that the concept was right-on for management and leadership too. Proper execution begins with the proper state of mind.

As we dive into the management concept of Gentle Pressure Relentlessly Applied, I encourage you to adopt the *proper state of mind.* If you do, you'll generally know how to respond in every management decision you face.

This book lays out many practical applications for this philosophy. That said, this book is not a specific prescription for your unique challenge, but more of a best-practice treatment plan that works in any change situation. You can be sure that you'll face something in your future career that's not specifically described here. No problem. The concepts work—and your *proper state of mind* will continue to serve you well. You can be confident. You can believe in yourself and this philosophy.

One of the lines in this poem is, "Success begins with a fellow's will." This remains as a powerful truth. Certainly, some people are born into success. But at some point, all of us must make the hard choice. We have to wake up, determined to achieve our goal.

To help with that process of adopting the right mindset to achieve your goals, I've created a commitment based on the model in this book:

The decisions I face daily, tempered by my commitment—

- *to be Gentle*
- *to create Pressure*
- *to lead Relentlessly*
- *as the person who Applies myself*

—will absolutely give me peace of mind, confidence in my approach, reinforcement of my relationships, and guaranteed success.

WHAT'S BEHIND THE PHRASE?

Gentle Pressure Relentlessly Applied is my business mantra. A sacred utterance. A phrase regularly repeated. The concept kept me focused and confident as I raised my children. It kept me moving forward as I led numerous teams. This concept has helped me be successful with many of my clients.

At first glance, it seems to need no explanation—and certainly not a whole book about it. But bear with me. This phrase contains elements of action, strategy, temperament, force, patience, and discipline. Each of these elements could be expanded upon in a book—and they have been.

These words aren't used tritely or conjured up only when a leader needs to check off a box of "used positive words." As leaders, many of us surround ourselves with key phrases that remind us how to lead, or motivate us when we need it most. These words can help us find our way through the fog, piloting the plane despite turbulence. They can help us trust our radar when we can't see clearly, so that we land safely at our destination with our entire team intact. And they can help our team engage in the right behaviors—like putting the oxygen masks on correctly!—so that they are contributors to the overall success.

I've used many of these guiding phrases in my life:

- "Opportunity is missed by most people because it is dressed in overalls and looks like work." — Thomas Edison

- "Motivation is the art of getting people to do what you want them to do because they want to do it." — Dwight Eisenhower
- "Fall down seven times. Stand up eight." —Zen proverb
- And of course, "Do or do not, there is no try." —Yoda

Throughout my life, I continue to return to this mantra: *Gentle Pressure Relentlessly Applied.*

- How do I get my kids to participate in yard work? Gentle Pressure Relentlessly Applied.
- How do I grow this underperforming business unit? Gentle Pressure Relentlessly Applied.
- How do I change the culture in my company? Gentle Pressure Relentlessly Applied.
- How do I develop my skills as a musician? Gentle Pressure Relentlessly Applied.

Throughout this process, the mantra has become a *process* for living and leading. Let's take a closer look at each component—which I will refer to as *themes*, since they subtly drive how the process moves.

Gentle

Any action you take as a leader affects your team. So the first theme word in this mantra (and the change-management process) is "Gentle." Let's explore what it means in the context of managing change.

*Gentle*ness guides our actions, reminding us that there are reactions. It reminds us that people respond based on their own motivations, opinions, and life experience. You can't just crash into their world without impacting it.

When you're the leader, remember to be gentle.

One of today's highest-valued attributes is *emotional intelligence*. The term originated with Peter Salavoy and John Mayer, two researchers who published a journal article on the topic in 1990. But most who follow its concepts think of Dan Goleman, an author who popularized the topic in 1995 with his book, *Emotional Intelligence* (Goleman 2022).

Besides being a buzzword you've probably heard from HR or your leadership team, what is emotional intelligence? While you could find many definitions, I see it as the internal force that allows us to manage our emotions—so we can exhibit empathy, communicate effectively (hint: listen a lot), and navigate conflict with grace. Emotional intelligence lets us recognize our reactions before they show to others, slowing down our thoughts and behaviors so we can respond effectively to improve a situation, not make it worse. After all, it's not just other people who have reactions; we have them too! But they don't need to derail us if we remember to be *gentle*.

When we exhibit a gentle approach in our communications and behaviors as a leader, it helps others to respond in kind. We diminish the likelihood of a reaction, if we slow down our own emotions and remain mindful of how we engage with others.

In the book, *Getting It Right When It Matters Most*, authors Tony Gambill and Scott Carbonara provide a model for managing our *moments that matter (MTMs)*—that is, those that are important (the outcome matters), complex (no simple solution exists), and relational (they involve others). Most organizational changes hit these three categories! After calibrating our outlook to slow our reactions, the authors explain what happens when we engage with someone else who may also have heightened emotions. "Think about threading a needle. Given good lighting and appropriate corrective lenses, most people can slip a small thread through the tiny eye of a needle when they are holding the thread. Now imagine threading a needle when you are holding the thread—and another person is holding the needle." They explain that during these crucial moments that require others to collaborate towards a goal, we must engage in actions and communication that create mutual respect. This is emotional intelligence in action (Gambill and Carbonara 2021).

Despite its critical nature, emotional intelligence seems to be increasingly rare. We're all programmed as human beings to protect ourselves against threats, even if only perceived. When our emotions tell us a threat exists, we are prone to fight, flee, or freeze. Yet none of these reactions are productive to leading a team through change—nor are they productive for employees.

It is this reaction that causes employees to hear the bad news within your change announcement:

- "We're merging with a larger company" becomes: My job may be eliminated.
- "We're getting a new leader" becomes: Great, now I have to learn how to please a new boss; what if I can't?

- "We're bringing in consultants to help us with our culture" becomes: So they are figuring out which one of us should be canned?
- "I need to talk to you about your project" becomes: So what are you unhappy with now?

If we can exhibit emotional intelligence in how we communicate and lead—which includes anticipating how someone else feels—we can help others navigate change instead of resisting it. We can stay a step ahead of any reactions, helping them never to occur.

Becoming aware of one's own level of emotional intelligence is difficult—yet paramount. After becoming aware, achieving that self-awareness might be one of hardest developmental steps one can take.

Our own change begins with the desire to be emotionally intelligent. That is, to understand the context of our actions, be sensitive to and curious about the emotions of those around us, and be empathetic to the experience of someone else. These are all applied through gentleness towards those we lead.

Gentleness shouldn't be confused with weakness. Being gentle requires extraordinary commitment. Gentleness requires focus, restraint, discipline, and intent.

Do you remember the first time you held an infant? I remember feeling an overwhelming sense of responsibility. I understood that this human's life was literally in my hands. I needed to be strong. I had to be accurate. I had to create a safe place. I wanted to do everything correctly and make no mistakes—because I understood the consequences. And because I wanted the child to remain calm and content, I did all of that with as much gentleness as I could muster.

Yet I also remained strong to this infant. I'd supply him with whatever he needed to thrive, without question. If someone were to threaten him, I'd protect him. If he grew into a child who needed my guidance and support, I'd gladly supply it.

As I continue to explain Gentle Pressure Relentlessly Applied, you will hear me talk about determination, intensity, force of will, even creating pain and discomfort. Remember where we started: gentle. Remember the first word: *gentle*. Remember that at your core—as a leader, parent, coach—you're charged with the care and respect of people.

Begin with *gentle*. Even when you're creating discomfort. Even when there is overreaction. Even when there are tears. Remember to be gentle.

Let's look at a few strategies on how to be gentle in the context of business, so we recognize it when we see it.

1. Tell the truth and tell it well. This is one of my favorite phrases to describe an emotionally intelligent leader. A gentle leader doesn't hide the truth so as not to hurt anyone. Doing so would create distrust and disharmony when the truth eventually comes out—and disruptive rumors in the meantime. Rather, a gentle leader is committed to sharing the truth—demonstrating trust in others to handle that truth and respond constructively.

Yet (and this is important!) this leader is also committed to speaking with love, dignity, and respect.

I've known lots of leaders who tell the truth! They say:

- "Dan, you don't look good in that suit. Whoever recommended you wear a turtleneck gave you bad advice!"
- "You'll never make it on your own. You don't have enough drive."
- "That was one of worst speeches I've ever heard. You lost the crowd in the first five minutes. What a waste of time."

Think about the intensity of emotion you may feel even thinking about negative words spoken against you. Do you ever find yourself riled up about something a colleague said about you, even when you are trying to sleep? Yet what if your boss praises you? Do you find yourself losing any sleep? It's unlikely you do. Research points to our inherent negativity bias, which makes us more apt to remember and react to negative words than positive. In fact, most of us can remember something mean we heard on the playground in grade school better than kind words spoken to us last night! In our emotional intelligence workshops, we teach that one minute of negative stimulus can take four hours to recover from. While we need to tell the truth to others when it matters, we also need to do so with respect.

Telling the truth well requires that you remove the negative emotion and judgment and simply state "what is." Communicate the facts about a change or situation, and allow people to have their own emotions. Focus on the behaviors you want to see, not on the faulty person you see in front of you. Doing so allows you to treat people with respect while still addressing the issue at hand. Here are some alternatives to the earlier examples:

- Issue silence about the turtleneck; it doesn't matter!
- "If you're interested in that leadership position one day, let's talk about what skills you can develop to move in that direction—and what you might need to change."
- "The premise of your speech was spot-on. I'd love to share some ideas to help your introduction, so you keep people engaged."

2. **Demonstrate self-control.** Jim Collins, in his book, *Good to Great*, describes his view of the ideal leader as a "Level Five" leader. He says this leader is "a paradoxical blend of professional will and personal humility." In other words, gentleness in leadership means you can keep your eye on the goal, the competition, and the progress—while also maintaining a humility that keeps perspective and relationships strong (Collins 2001).

3. **Show curiosity.** This is as simple as paying attention to those on your team and asking questions about them. Sadly, the busyness of business coupled with the competitive nature of leadership has reduced or removed this very important attribute from too many people. One of the greatest gifts you can give someone is to just listen to them. Take cues from their environment and what they talk about when they

have free time, and be curious. Hint: ask questions. Here are a few easy ones:

- "How was your weekend?" (Then listen, and learn something about them and their interests. Maybe they like polka dancing, or raising show pigs, or something else that makes them light up. Now you can ask them about that next time you see them!)
- "What did you think about that lunch-and-learn? Anything stand out to you?" (You may learn about their priorities and values, ideas for the future, and more.)
- "How did you feel that meeting went?" (You may gauge their response to corporate communications or get new ideas you hadn't considered.)

Think about it. When was the last time someone actually listened to you? What did this look like? I mean that they were present. They made eye contact. They didn't interrupt. They listened. How can you provide this to those you lead?

Watch a toddler sometime. Most of their life is spent around adults—people who are smarter, busier, and much taller than they are. They are rarely listened to or given full focus. Oh sure, when they were infants, they got all the attention. But those days are gone. Now, they're given toys on the floor (or god-forbid, an iPad!) and left to entertain themselves. But if—just if—some random adult gets down on one knee and looks in the toddler's eyes and stays at that level with the child, you'll see a transformation. The child isn't used to this type of attention and usually relishes it. They can't believe their good luck—someone is giving them full attention! I've seen children in this situation actually hold the adult's face to keep their attention. They don't want it to end.

Sadly, most of us go through too much of our lives without any focused curiosity on us either. This is why of the best steps toward gentleness is simple: be curious.

As we progress through the Gentle Pressure Relentlessly Applied process, we're going to be introducing some "power words": *pressure, relentless, applied*. Don't forget where we started. Because leadership involves people, we must also be *gentle*.

Gentle Pressure

In physics, *pressure* is expressed as "Force per unit area": $P=F/A$. Pressure is usually a continuous, ongoing amount of force. The word "pressure" expresses a long-term, intense effort.

- "I have high blood pressure."
- "Stop pressuring me."
- "She was pressuring him to quit."
- "The daily pressure of his job was starting to wear on him."
- "You should apply pressure to the wound to stop the bleeding."

How does pressure apply to change? When you intend to lead change, you must commit to take action (apply force) over a longer period of time. It's this commitment to action that creates the difference.

My friend, Rich Wills—the former owner of Fit Niche, a running store in western Florida—says that almost anyone can develop the ability to run for thirty minutes a day, if they follow his disciplined approach. His plan sounds simple: On the first day of your thirty-day plan, simply run for one minute. On the second day, run two minutes. On the third day, run three minutes. Increase your time by one minute each day through the thirty days, and you will have developed the muscle strength needed to run thirty minutes. You also will have prevented any overuse injuries, which is the most common obstacle new runners face.

Many people who start out on this plan become impatient. Since they are able to run more than one minute on the first day, they do so. Usually, they extend themselves too much. Then they are too tired or sore from the first run, and they skip a day or two to recover. Before long, the entire idea of a thirty-minute run is forgotten and abandoned. It's difficult to stay focused and committed to the consistent approach necessary to achieve long-term success.

I've experienced this challenge with long projects as well. This is my second book. The first book I wrote, *ORBiT: The Art and Science of Influence*, was completed in 2017 after a decade of failed attempts. In the years before this, I would start to write (without a plan), and before long, the general disorganization of the process would catch up to my efforts.

I'd lose momentum and eventually end the project. But with ORBiT, I did things differently:

- First, I used a writing software called Scrivener, which let me organize the entire project at once.
- Next, I bought headphones and wore them to listen to "focus music," which helped me concentrate.
- I set a deadline (November 22) which I announced to my family and coworkers.
- Then I set aside a time every morning (6:00 a.m.) to write, and I wrote in the same place at the same time every day.
- Finally, I set a word goal for each day (750). I made an agreement with myself that I couldn't end the session until I hit that goal.
- Once I'd completed the full draft, I hired an editor to help me polish and complete the book for publication.

By creating this structure for myself, and adding the additional "peer pressure" of making myself accountable to others, I systematically achieved the goal of finishing the book. I didn't always enjoy hearing the alarm at 6:00 a.m. Some days, it was brutally difficult to create even 750 words. Occasionally, it was a challenge to smile when a family member asked, "How's the book coming along?" I felt *pressure*. But I'd created this structure for just that reason. This pressure created a favorable result.

Similar to this example, you'll see in later chapters that *metrics create the pressure*. As you lead your team toward change, you'll learn to identify the correct metric in order to create pressure.

Creating pressure is absolutely required in order to generate change. This is why the education system creates standards for retention and performance. A grade of 93 to 100 percent is an A; 85 to 92 is a B; and so on until you reach 65, which is the lowest score you can receive and still pass a course. These metrics create *pressure*.

If you want to be accepted at Harvard University, you'll need an SAT score of at least 1460 (among many other measurable criteria). When a Harvard-bound student takes the SAT, that number creates the pressure to perform during the test.

Pressure is expressed and measured in many ways. There's water pressure, air pressure, atmospheric pressure, surface pressure, etc. In all cases, these pressures are expressed as a unit of force. In other words, we can ask and answer: how much force is being applied?

- We measure a tire's air pressure in pounds.
- Blood pressure measures how much pressure is exerted by blood while flowing through the blood vessels.

As we apply this concept to the management of people, it may seem odd to use "force" in the language of leadership. Organizations have worked for centuries to force people into certain behavioral changes. Some have been well intended:

- Societal rules, for example, help maintain order and safety.

- Guidelines for education are developed and enforced to build standards and measurements for mental development.

In other cases, pressure and force have been turned into manipulative and subjective efforts to subvert an individual's independence. When a manager does this, you will likely see the following:

- You'll hear them making sarcastic comments in the interest of shaming people into performing.
- You'll see them grow frustrated and lose their temper.
- You'll see them attempt rewards or punishments as a method of control.
- Mostly you'll see them being ineffective.

In your role leading a team, the application of force will be one of your most challenging choices. You'll need to assess: *When do I relax and allow people to fail in the interest of discovery? When do I step in and exert force to change the outcome?* It can feel daunting to hit that balance, but we'll introduce a method to do so. Hint: in order to create the ideal environment for healthy pressure, you'll need to select and apply the best metric to achieve the results you want.

You've likely seen leaders who have resorted to their own methods to exert pressure (without metrics), such as in the examples just shared. Just this week, I was meeting with a business owner in retail who was frustrated with her team. Most of her staff were underperforming in their sales results.

The company was decreasing in sales performance overall—and here's the kicker—many of her team members were complaining to her that they weren't being paid enough! Low sales, company performance in decline, dissatisfaction from the staff about their compensation—you can imagine the effect this had on company morale!

My interaction with this owner went something like this:

Me: "Sarah, what is the standard for sales performance in your store?"
Sarah: "What do you mean?"
Me: "Have you told your staff what you expect in terms of their sales results—either hourly or daily?"
Sarah: "Mercy, no! They would never go for that."
Me: "So they have no expectation, no standard of performance, no pressure to perform, and you're the person solely responsible for their job satisfaction and compensation increase? This is not a win-win!"
Sarah: [Silence.]

Sarah wanted to change her sales results, but she was attempting to do so without any metrics—or standards of performance—to create pressure.

In another recent conversation, a client (multi-store retailer) in the bicycle industry was bemoaning his increasing inventory loss and believed that it had something to do with their inter-store transfer process.

Me:	"Do you have a process for transfers between stores?
Ken:	"Yes, of course."
Me:	"Is it documented?"
Ken:	"Yes, it's recorded on video and written in our Google Drive."
Me:	"What are the metrics associated with the transfer process?"
Ken:	"I don't understand."
Me:	"What parts of the transfer process are measured (number of items transferred out or received, etc.)?"
Ken:	"None." (Sigh.)
Me:	"Are you certain everyone knows the process and is following it correctly?"
Ken:	"How would I know that?"
Me:	"How many times has your training video been viewed?"
Ken:	(After a quick check…) "Six." (Shakes his head and sheepishly smiles.)

Now let me ask you:

- What are you trying to change that has thus far been unsuccessful?
- What metrics have you applied to the process?

- Where's the pressure?
- So what do you think is the next step?

We will explore how to exert the right type and amount of pressure as we move forward in this book.

Gentle Pressure Relentlessly

Constant, incessant, oppressive, showing no sign of letting up = *relentless*.

In our mantra and process, *relentlessly* denotes your force of will. The root word *relent* means to soften or reduce. It's described as "the notion of a heart melting." Well, relent-*LESS* will have none of that! There will be no relenting, no softening, no letting up. Instead, we decide: *I am intent. I am determined. I am firm. I am relentless.*

When you lead change, you will be incurring some resistance. When dealing with people (employees, coworkers, children, customers), you should remember that no one inherently likes change—even if they think or say they do. Sure, we might like the change of getting a raise or a surprise dessert when we didn't expect it. But most changes come with some loss—of familiarity or routine. Self-determination theory suggests that we may feel reactive when we perceive a threat to our autonomy, relatedness, or certainty (also called the ARC model)—which are all at play during change. Change can threaten us. We resist it, and in many cases, we will go to great extremes to avoid it. With so much pressure *resisting* change, it's easy for you as a leader to simply take the path of least resistance. And it's easy for your team and employees to do the same. Often, this is where movement toward change comes to an end (Deci and Ryan 1985).

From your own experience, how have you observed people as behaving when they are resisting change? Think about that for a minute or two.

Here's my list:

- People often resort to tears if no other option seems to work. This is often an attempt (often unconscious) to divert attention to their emotions, rather than to the topic of the change. (I'm not dismissing a need to cry; this is a statement about crying in order to avoid the change.)
- Some like to divert attention by "fogging" when confronted with the change (directing the conversation to another issue altogether).
- Shouting works for others.
- I've seen people fake illness to avoid change.
- Believe it or not, I've witnessed employees (and my children) pretend they didn't hear the instruction!
- One of the best (easiest to fly under the radar) methods I've seen is to pretend to go along with the change—but secretly work to sabotage the new approach.

I've come to believe that in some cases, people will work harder to avoid change than they would need to if they simply accepted the change!

Because of this reality, YOU MUST BE RELENTLESS. In other words, be persistent, constant, consistent, nonstop, never-ending, steady, continuing, unwavering, sustained, determined, purposeful, even stubborn.

Do these words describe you now? If not, how do you develop "steadiness" or "purposefulness"? How do you develop *RELENTLESS* as an attribute?

Following are some tips on how to be relentless, and we will explore the application of this theme more as we get further into the book. These are important concepts for you as a leader, and most of them can also be helpful for those you lead:

- **Make the decision to be relentless.** You will be a determined, purposeful leader. Write it down. Say it out loud. Tell someone. Make it a real goal for yourself.
- **Be clear about your reason why.** This one is vital. Humans have been known to go to extraordinary lengths to accomplish something they truly believe in. What is that thing for you?
- **Take care of yourself.** It's a fact that you are not at your best when you're tired, hungry, or stressed. One way to remain determined, focused, and steady is to simply stay rested, relaxed, and healthy. (This probably sounds like the advice your mom gave you. It turns out she was right, and research backs her up.)
- **Create discipline about your time management.** When you're rushed and "out of time," you will end up distracted, stressed, and ineffective.
- **Stay focused on the end result you want—and why it's important.** In fact, the more you can picture—

actually visualize—your intended result, the more likely you are to achieve it.

Gentle Pressure Relentlessly Applied

Now it makes sense, right? When you put all these words together—*gentle, pressure, relentlessly*—you really don't have anything cohesive until you add the word, *applied*.

Applied is defined as: "put to practical use or brought into action." Applied is actually the opposite of abstract or theoretical. Once something is applied, it's real. It's being used.

If you're a leader who is in the business of change, you want real, not theoretical, results. And you want real, not theoretical, change.

Organizations often fall short on the execution of their change intentions. I've seen leaders talk about a change for years, but never implement it. Eventually, employees stop believing it will happen—and they stop believing their leaders at all.

As a leader, you will have to move from the theoretical to the practical. You will have to take action and *apply* the pressure. Yes, *applied* is referring to *pressure*.

This is where those without the force of will are going to have a tough time. Applying pressure is not for those who are casual about change. If your results are optional, there's no need to insist on action. But if you are reading this book, I'm assuming your results are not optional; pressure is necessary. In fact, only those change initiatives that include an element of pressure will get results.

What does *applied pressure* look like?

- It's the parent who insists on enforcing the bedtime rules in the presence of intense crying and debate.
- It's the supervisor who disciplines the employee after two tardies.
- It's the pet owner who establishes a systematic formula for meals, playtime, and sleep.
- It's the person who changes their habits due to a determination to lose weight, eat healthy, and exercise regularly.
- It's the high school graduate who takes night classes at a community college so she can work to pay for her own education.
- It's the coach who insists the team runs just five more laps after an exhausting practice.

You might think some of these look like consequences. You might state that all of these require discipline. You might not know where to begin, especially if your work (or home or athletic team or fill-in-the-blank) culture has languished in allowing people *not* to perform.

Many leaders won't do these things, because they require the application (and reinforcement) of a plan. If others are involved (the employee, pet, children, team members), it's unpopular to require them to do something they wouldn't ordinarily do. This resistance applies to internal changes too, within ourselves. Sure, the *idea* of losing weight sounds good in theory, but achieving it is difficult.

Meaningful change requires applying *pressure*. So many won't do it.

For example, of course the *concept* of having all of your employees keep to the posted schedule without tardiness would be ideal. But to achieve that means that someone will have to apply pressure (yes, in the form of consequences) to employees who are late. And that is going to create some discomfort, and maybe worse, so many supervisors won't do it.

Ideally, a coach would want the team to be in top physical shape for the season. However, requiring the team members to work hard at physical fitness will require applying pressure on a consistent basis, so many coaches won't do it.

Losing weight sounds easy—on New Year's Eve. You are all about change, and you even buy new running shoes and shorts. When New Year's Day rolls around, the slate is clean, and you get started by heading to the gym early. But how about a week later, when your regular Friday night group invites you for cocktails and appetizers? Will you apply pressure to maintain your plan? Or will you stop fighting the resistance you feel to slip back into your old routine—the one where change fizzles into oblivion as the bourbon settles in your belly?

Applying pressure (expectations, guidelines, standards, extra work, schedules) won't be met with unanimous acceptance. So how will that play out? There you will stand—the *one* person insisting on behavior change—while your children, employees, or team are displaying all the actions of outrage, oppression, and revolt.

Once you have decided on a change, in order to lead others through it so that you won't end up on the finish line alone (or sleeping in the bushes from fatigue), you'll have to be determined. You will have to be certain. I say you have to be *bulletproof.*

There is a classic scene in the movie, *Miracle*, which depicts this point. The actor Kurt Russell portrays Herb Brooks, the real-life coach of the 1980 US Hockey team, which won the gold medal after the famed "Miracle on Ice" game.

After a particularly poor effort from his team—and a full day of playing hockey—the coach demanded that the team go back out on the ice for an hour of "Herbies," an intense conditioning drill. The team wasn't practicing with their sticks, pucks, or nets. The players were just skating back and forth on the ice, in wind sprints.

After each drill, the coach continued to shout, "Again!" The team—and the other coaches—were outraged and exhausted. Even the arena shut off the lights. Still, Coach Brooks applied the pressure.

To this day, the players on that team contend that those drills are a primary reason they won the gold. They felt they were in better shape than any other team, and that was proven by outscoring all other teams 16–3 in the third period, when other players ran out of energy.

It wasn't popular at the time, but despite the discomfort and the complaints, Herb Brooks applied pressure. That's what it takes to create change.

PART TWO

FROM CONCEPT TO APPLICATION

GENTLE PRESSURE RELENTLESSLY APPLIED

CHAPTER 3

A CLOSER LOOK AT THE INFOGRAPHIC

FOR MANY OF us, just hearing the phrase, "Gentle Pressure Relentlessly Applied" is all we need to understand its meaning and how to apply it. That was my experience. As soon as I was introduced to it, I immediately applied it to my management style. I've often quoted it, taught it, and reflected on it.

But in the twenty-eight years or so since I first heard it, I've still had times when I struggled to implement the concepts effectively. If I was unsuccessful as a manager, I never questioned the concept's validity or purpose—but I knew I'd missed something in the implementation.

So, upon realizing this, I took the time to define the implementation—as detailed in the rest of this book.

Leading change is more than an ideology. Ultimately, it comes down to tactics, disciplined behavior, relationship-building, math, and a bulletproof focus on the end result. Learning and applying these details will be key for you in managing change.

The infographic before this chapter is your bird's-eye guide. If you're experiencing a breakdown and not getting the results you want, look at the four *phases*, which again are:

1. Agreement on Approach
2. Metrics for Assurance
3. Training and Coaching
4. Culture of Accountability

Which of them is the root of your failure? Which one *didn't* you do? This infographic—along with the tactics I'll share throughout the rest of this book—can help you diagnose the problem.

Each phase also comes with a word which is your desired outcome from that phase. In this chapter, we will explore how each of the themes and phases work together to create outcomes—and drive change. In later chapters, we will dive deeper into how to achieve each phase.

If you want to start a great effort and make *absolutely* sure that you achieve your result, then follow the phases in the rest of the book exactly. You'll get what you want—as illustrated by the outcomes associated with each. The Gentle Pressure Relentlessly Applied process will be presented in such a way that any leader with focus and commitment can implement it.

FOCUS ON THE FIRST QUADRANT: AGREEMENT ON APPROACH

Leading change includes a human component. Others must join you—buying into the change—for it to be successful. Where do you start? You must begin by implementing phase one: securing an Agreement on Approach. This means that you and your team must understand the reason for the change (including *what's in it for me*) and agree on how you will operate through it. You ultimately must align not only on the guiding principles of expected behaviors during the change, but also what will be required once the change is in effect.

If you're implementing a new software system, for example, you can guide people in understanding why it's important. Maybe the old one will no longer support your customers as you grow, so it's needed to keep the company strong and competitive. Doing so will ensure growth—benefiting employees through job security. Once the "why" is clear, the team can align around the change and learn everything necessary to implement it. When the change is underway, the team also needs alignment—around operating differently within the new system, while engaging in new tasks and habits.

But the process of acquiring alignment must be done gently. These are people. Your team. And they must make this choice freely—not under duress or out of fear. Consider their potential threats (including to their autonomy, relatedness, and certainty), and thread the needle of change with them. They may be afraid the new system will be hard to learn, for example, putting them out of a job. Reassure them that you will train them fully (then back that up; see the next points!).

When done properly, you'll achieve *alignment*—one of the strongest words in the context of a team. Picture a rowing crew. Every team member pulls in perfect time, performing their task in perfect alignment with everyone in the boat. This precise alignment maximizes effectiveness and results. If you've ever been on this type of team, you know there's nothing like the harmony and peak performance achieved.

On the flip side, if you've ever had a car with tires out of alignment, you know the downfalls. One tire pulls unevenly, threatening to veer the car off the road without self-correcting work from the driver. The vehicle experiences wear and tear as its steering system isn't smoothly operating. This isn't unlike some experiences in leadership—where some team members are pulling against you while you try to steer straight!

Creating alignment is always the first step in any change initiative. Without alignment, you can't move forward without distraction or even sabotage. With alignment, you can shoot for any destination.

FOCUS ON THE SECOND QUADRANT: METRICS FOR ASSURANCE

As we've discussed, the metrics around a change create the pressure, because those results give visibility/transparency into progress. Without the correct metrics, we lose the pressure. Without metrics, what do we have instead? Opinion. Emotion. No accountability. Know what you are changing, and define what it will look like when you get there—using measurable outcomes. This is why phase two involves implementing Metrics for Assurance.

FOCUS ON THE THIRD QUADRANT: TRAINING AND COACHING

As we've discussed, relentlessness is a word we frequently hear used to describe "the pursuit of excellence," "the commitment to winning," or "achieving perfection." This is why the athletes we admire—the ones who overcome obstacles and achieve success—are tireless (relentless) in their learning, practicing, and training. It's how most of us get better. We develop skills (the outcome) after implementing phase three: Training and Coaching.

That relentlessness never shows stronger than when an underdog sweeps a competition. Consider the thoroughbred, Rich Strike, who won the 2022 Kentucky Derby despite 80:1 odds against him. The owner stated in a media interview after the race that the trainer knew they might have a special horse, so they decided to back into the Derby—optimizing the colt's training to be at his prime that day, if he had the opportunity. "We went to the calendar, first Saturday in May," owner Rick Dawson stated. "We backed up every five weeks from there, and we started picking races so that when we got here, we wouldn't be tired. We'd be improving." When another horse was scratched, Rich Strike stepped into place, because he was ready. His team had trained him for that moment, and despite any past losses or dismal odds, he stunned the field and millions of onlookers with a sweeping victory (ESPN 2022).

Having a well-trained team of performers will be crucial for any task you attempt—especially around a change.

FOCUS ON THE FOURTH QUADRANT: CULTURE OF ACCOUNTABILITY

It all comes together here: culture, accountability, integrity. Ultimately, as a leader your integrity will be measured by the culture you create and nurture. That's why the final word in the mantra is *applied*. When you implement phase four—a Culture of Accountability—you will achieve the outcome of integrity.

Again and again, we see that those who achieve the desired results are those who seek this accountability—applying everything they've learned. Imagine if the owner of Rich Strike hadn't been enthusiastic to support the training of this long-shot horse? But he was, and he fostered a culture of accountability to apply everything necessary to achieve those results. He had integrity to seek the outcome, and he encouraged it in others.

Those who make the effort, call the meeting, or complete the to-do list are those who achieve greatness. They don't just talk about concepts; they apply them. When a team does this in unison (aligned to a goal, training for its outcome), nothing can stop them.

Thomas Edison knew something about applying effort to get results. He said, "Opportunity is missed by most people, because it is dressed in overalls and looks like work."

Now let's go back to the infographic that appeared before the chapter. Notice that at the top are two words: Leading Change.

The themes and phases are put here in order for you to achieve the outcomes—of *alignment, transparency, skills*, and *integrity*—and accomplish great change. What is it that you believe needs change? What great effort are you committed to?

Maybe—

- Your team is charged with developing new software for security or communication effectiveness.
- You just inherited your father's highly successful auto dealership, and now it's your turn to lead this family business into the future.
- Your nonprofit works to improve education for those with less opportunity.
- You're a bicycle retailer working to add more bike lanes in your city.
- You're a soccer coach trying to make it to the regional finals for the first time in a decade.
- Your company has just come off its worst quarter in five years. The board has charged you with making big changes and achieving better results.
- _____(insert your change here).

Fill in the blank. But just picture the new result you want. Because if it is *you* who is leading change, it will be you who must be out front. *Applying*, being *relentless*, feeling *pressure*—and exerting it. All the while, you'll be finding the emotional intelligence to be *gentle*.

Sure, it may well be the challenge of your life. The results will be worth it.

In the future chapters, we will delve more deeply into how to implement each phase associated with Gentle Pressure Relentlessly Applied, to guide you in your change. But first, we will explore each of the four outcomes in a bit more detail, so that you have those goals in mind as you lead your change.

CHAPTER 4

"IF RUNNING IS DIFFICULT, RUN MORE"— FOCUSING ON YOUR OUTCOMES

Now that we've explored how the themes and phases of Gentle Pressure Relentlessly Applied work together, it's time to dive a bit deeper into the outcomes of each phase—*alignment, transparency, skills,* and *integrity*—as you prepare for your change process. This chapter will touch on these outcomes as they apply to each of the four phases. (Later, we will dive into how to engage in each of these four phases within your change initiative.)

ALIGNMENT

My friend, Steffen Root, owner of Berkshire Bike and Board in western Massachusetts, tells me that *alignment* might be my favorite word. Apparently, I use it all the time. As a consultant and business owner, I'm not surprised. I've seen the disasters that occur when teams are not in alignment. I've also been inspired by seeing the incredible accomplishments of a team that is in alignment.

So when you're not getting results with your team, I suggest you start here by simply asking yourself: *is my team in alignment?* You probably have a gut-level response to that question. But since we're all about the metrics, I'll further explore the outcome of *alignment* in this chapter, so you can fully understand how it works—and if you have it. If you don't, we'll explore how to achieve it.

Look at the infographic again. Remember, *alignment* comes from an Agreement on Approach, and it's achieved through the theme of being *gentle* as a change leader. Securing alignment is a gentle process. People will align most powerfully when they see it as optional. Alignment by force (fear of losing one's job, for example) might work short-term, but it doesn't bring about the Culture of Accountability that is your goal.

Let's take a closer look at the power of alignment—and how to achieve it in your Agreement on Approach.

The Mann Group conducts about twenty strategic plans each year for our clients and partners. It's the first kind of project we offered when the company began, and we continue to do it to this day. On the first day of the planning meeting, in the first hour, we announce the rules for the meetings. Some organizations call these guiding principles. Consider them like rules of engagement describing how your group will operate. Some change initiatives have their own guiding principles. In our strategic sessions, we introduce and apply ten of them.

By far, the most important rule is how the group makes a decision:

- Decisions of the group are made by *alignment*.

What does this mean? It means we don't use a majority-rule vote. We don't use passive *consensus*. Decisions must have active *alignment*.

What's the difference? Leaders who say they make decisions by consensus may be fooling themselves. Over time, consensus can lead to a passive decision-making process where some team members give up sharing their opinions out of frustration from never being heard. Alignment requires every person to agree to the decision, *as if they had come up with it themselves*. It's much more intentional.

Let me explain further. When the group is deciding on an initiative or a new direction for the organization, *everyone* on the team must *fully agree as if they had come up with the idea themselves!* When it's decision time, we go around the room and ask everyone: "Are you aligned?" (This is a bit like asking if someone sitting in the exit row of the airplane is willing and able to assist in case of an emergency—providing a preliminary Metric for Assurance.) Asking for alignment up front means no person can come back at a later time and say, "Well, I was never in favor of this decision."

We ask the question sincerely, as this is the time to provide pushback. Any objections can be raised, which allows a team to improve a plan—or their own mindsets—until alignment is unanimous. If someone in the group is opposed to the initiative, they must speak up. In other words—and here's the challenge—any one person can prevent a decision from being made.

Now you may be thinking to yourself, *how do you ever get anything done?* I'll explain next steps in just a moment. But here's the reason we use this decision-making protocol: we'd rather have all our decisions made with the full alignment of the entire group, than to have any decisions made which some members of the team are opposed to. Why? Because we know the power of alignment—as well as the pull of misalignment.

Again, think of your car with one wheel out of alignment. Even if you ignore it, it will constantly pull your vehicle towards the gutter. Address it now, so you can travel straight to your destination.

How do we pull off this alignment? We have four prerequisites:

1. The leader of this team (owner, CEO, president) must also value the power of alignment and be willing to prioritize it.
2. We must have the right people in the room. The right people are decision-makers who can work in the best

interest of the organization—by proxy—instead of based on their own agenda.
3. Everyone must commit to investigate and offer follow-up when one person offers an objection.
4. All team members must commit to respectful, active listening with each other.

How do you provide follow-up? We also have a process for that. If one team member can't align, that person must set about to convince the rest of the members of their point of view.

Let me ask you, have you ever been in a strategic meeting and watched as the entire room was swayed into the wrong direction? Have you tried to convince them otherwise? Were you the only person who was right? Of course!

Sometimes only one person in the room has the best point of view. So we allow that single person the opportunity to convince remaining members of the team of their point of view. They can offer some new information. They can present some new perspective. Maybe they're successful. If so, we align to this new direction. Decision made—and alignment achieved.

But maybe the one person isn't successful at persuasion. It's now incumbent on the other members of the group to gently and respectfully convince the one person of the group's point of view. Remember, respectful listening is key. If successful, the one person has the opportunity to change their mind, shifting their paradigm and joining the others in an aligned decision.

If neither side can affect a change, the group agrees to a twenty-four-hour cooling off period. The group reconvenes on the topic at hand and goes back through the same process stated above. This continues until full alignment is reached. This "deadline" is important, so that decisions don't get defaulted upon until a vague, unknown future date. Organizations that don't put a time limit on making decisions tend to stall—or avoid change altogether. This also prevents any one person from using the rule of alignment as an excuse to filibuster to avoid any decision from being made.

In more than twenty-five years of working under this decision-making rule, I have never seen any group that didn't reach alignment, usually within the first twenty-four hours.

Why does this work?

- Everyone in the room knows they won't be forced into a decision they can't endorse fully.
- Everyone knows they have the power of veto.
- Everyone knows what's at risk if they can't align (more meetings!).
- Everyone knows that their integrity requires that they can't reverse their position at some later, convenient time.
- Everyone now understands the value of alignment.

This may sound risky to you. If so, look closely at your team. Would your team members agree to the four prerequisites listed earlier in the chapter for working this way?

Gaining alignment doesn't mean that a team member might not express dissatisfaction with a direction later. But if they do, you can gently remind them of the decision made and the principles guiding the change. This should be enough to get a committed team member back in alignment. Think of this like hitting a rock on the road, which temporarily jostles the vehicle. If the alignment is strong enough, it should withstand any temporary and small obstacle.

This method works. It builds powerful teams. It reinforces alignment. It's gentle and respectful of everyone on the team.

Here's what you create as byproducts of (and contributors to) an aligned team:

- Momentum
- Trust
- Confidence
- Synergy
- Energy
- Direction

And, most of all:

- The focused power of everyone's energy toward your goal!

It's no wonder alignment is one of my favorite words. With it, anything is possible. Without it, well, you may be in for a tough, uphill climb to your goal.

The alignment method isn't only used in business process. I would direct your attention to the US legal system and the method that a jury uses to make a decision in a federal trial—where the stakes are high. A human being is on trial. They have been accused of a crime, and their future (and sometimes their life) hangs in the balance. A randomly selected group of twelve citizens is directed to determine the truth from all the evidence—and decide about this person's fate. The prosecution makes the case against the defendant. The defense team presents their evidence to the contrary. Once this process is complete, the jury retires to a private room where they review, discuss, argue, debate, and work in whatever way they choose to secure a *unanimous* decision about the person who is on trial.

What a curious process! These twelve random jurors are charged with deciding someone's fate, using only the information presented by the attorneys. Their decision-making method isn't a democracy. The decision is too important to be left to "majority rule." The decision isn't weighted towards jurors with more education or wealth. Every person on the jury must fully agree with the decision: guilty or innocent.

In some important cases, the attorneys will poll the jurors, asking each one to state, individually, their agreement with the group's choice. Imagine the pressure of sitting in a courtroom—in front of the defendant, the judge, the media, and the defendant's family—and being asked, "Do you agree that this defendant is guilty as charged?" In effect, the jury members are being asked to show alignment to a decision.

As you lead a team, you'll want each member aligned. Failure to ensure this can guarantee frustration at best and total

failure at worst. The importance of securing this alignment is directly tied to the importance of your mission—which again points to your *why*.

- What is this great thing you have to achieve?
- What is the inspiring accomplishment that you intend to bring to reality?
- What is it that you have dedicated yourself to?
- Will you leave it to chance—simply hoping that everyone is on board?

Alignment must be your only option.

TRANSPARENCY

The outcome achieved through Metrics for Assurance is *transparency*. I could just as accurately name it lucidity, clarity, intelligibility, or thinking clearly.

Wikipedia says this about transparency: "Transparency, as used in science, engineering, business, the humanities, and in other social contexts is operating in such a way that it is easy for others to see what actions are performed. Transparency implies openness, communication and accountability."

Again, the context for the discussion of these concepts is *leading change*. When something is changing, metrics give us the ability to measure that change. In my Gentle Pressure Relentlessly Applied model, the *metrics provide assurance that we are making progress.* That's why the associated outcome is transparency. We want the results to be easily identified. We want there to be no room for interpretation.

The transparency (visibility) that metrics offer will give you many additional benefits:

- Your team can see through the improving metrics that their efforts are working. This provides inspiration, increasing commitment, and momentum.
- You can identify quickly that your approach is the right one, validating the process for future use and training.
- You can also see if the approach needs correcting. If you're getting no results, perhaps you should reconsider your approach—making changes in time to still achieve your desired results.
- You reduce the possibility of emotionally-based interpretation. The results speak for themselves.
- You build trust when your team knows that decisions are made based on ongoing, measurable results—not whims. This trust trickles into other areas of leadership. As David Horsager, author of *The Trust Edge*, states, "Whether you are a student or a CEO, a teacher or a parent, a politician or a nurse, trust multiples influence and impact" (Horsager 2009, 8).

Look at examples from this in everyday life:

- You child complains of a headache. You grab a thermometer and take her temperature. It's not that you doubt your child's story, but the metrics (temperature) give you visibility into what had previously been a child's perception. A temperature of

failure at worst. The importance of securing this alignment is directly tied to the importance of your mission—which again points to your *why*.

- What is this great thing you have to achieve?
- What is the inspiring accomplishment that you intend to bring to reality?
- What is it that you have dedicated yourself to?
- Will you leave it to chance—simply hoping that everyone is on board?

Alignment must be your only option.

TRANSPARENCY

The outcome achieved through Metrics for Assurance is *transparency*. I could just as accurately name it lucidity, clarity, intelligibility, or thinking clearly.

Wikipedia says this about transparency: "Transparency, as used in science, engineering, business, the humanities, and in other social contexts is operating in such a way that it is easy for others to see what actions are performed. Transparency implies openness, communication and accountability."

Again, the context for the discussion of these concepts is *leading change*. When something is changing, metrics give us the ability to measure that change. In my Gentle Pressure Relentlessly Applied model, the *metrics provide assurance that we are making progress*. That's why the associated outcome is transparency. We want the results to be easily identified. We want there to be no room for interpretation.

The transparency (visibility) that metrics offer will give you many additional benefits:

- Your team can see through the improving metrics that their efforts are working. This provides inspiration, increasing commitment, and momentum.
- You can identify quickly that your approach is the right one, validating the process for future use and training.
- You can also see if the approach needs correcting. If you're getting no results, perhaps you should reconsider your approach—making changes in time to still achieve your desired results.
- You reduce the possibility of emotionally-based interpretation. The results speak for themselves.
- You build trust when your team knows that decisions are made based on ongoing, measurable results—not whims. This trust trickles into other areas of leadership. As David Horsager, author of *The Trust Edge*, states, "Whether you are a student or a CEO, a teacher or a parent, a politician or a nurse, trust multiples influence and impact" (Horsager 2009, 8).

Look at examples from this in everyday life:

- You child complains of a headache. You grab a thermometer and take her temperature. It's not that you doubt your child's story, but the metrics (temperature) give you visibility into what had previously been a child's perception. A temperature of

failure at worst. The importance of securing this alignment is directly tied to the importance of your mission—which again points to your *why*.

- What is this great thing you have to achieve?
- What is the inspiring accomplishment that you intend to bring to reality?
- What is it that you have dedicated yourself to?
- Will you leave it to chance—simply hoping that everyone is on board?

Alignment must be your only option.

TRANSPARENCY

The outcome achieved through Metrics for Assurance is *transparency*. I could just as accurately name it lucidity, clarity, intelligibility, or thinking clearly.

Wikipedia says this about transparency: "Transparency, as used in science, engineering, business, the humanities, and in other social contexts is operating in such a way that it is easy for others to see what actions are performed. Transparency implies openness, communication and accountability."

Again, the context for the discussion of these concepts is *leading change*. When something is changing, metrics give us the ability to measure that change. In my Gentle Pressure Relentlessly Applied model, the *metrics provide assurance that we are making progress*. That's why the associated outcome is transparency. We want the results to be easily identified. We want there to be no room for interpretation.

The transparency (visibility) that metrics offer will give you many additional benefits:

- Your team can see through the improving metrics that their efforts are working. This provides inspiration, increasing commitment, and momentum.
- You can identify quickly that your approach is the right one, validating the process for future use and training.
- You can also see if the approach needs correcting. If you're getting no results, perhaps you should reconsider your approach—making changes in time to still achieve your desired results.
- You reduce the possibility of emotionally-based interpretation. The results speak for themselves.
- You build trust when your team knows that decisions are made based on ongoing, measurable results—not whims. This trust trickles into other areas of leadership. As David Horsager, author of *The Trust Edge*, states, "Whether you are a student or a CEO, a teacher or a parent, a politician or a nurse, trust multiples influence and impact" (Horsager 2009, 8).

Look at examples from this in everyday life:

- You child complains of a headache. You grab a thermometer and take her temperature. It's not that you doubt your child's story, but the metrics (temperature) give you visibility into what had previously been a child's perception. A temperature of

failure at worst. The importance of securing this alignment is directly tied to the importance of your mission—which again points to your *why*.

- What is this great thing you have to achieve?
- What is the inspiring accomplishment that you intend to bring to reality?
- What is it that you have dedicated yourself to?
- Will you leave it to chance—simply hoping that everyone is on board?

Alignment must be your only option.

TRANSPARENCY

The outcome achieved through Metrics for Assurance is *transparency*. I could just as accurately name it lucidity, clarity, intelligibility, or thinking clearly.

Wikipedia says this about transparency: "Transparency, as used in science, engineering, business, the humanities, and in other social contexts is operating in such a way that it is easy for others to see what actions are performed. Transparency implies openness, communication and accountability."

Again, the context for the discussion of these concepts is *leading change*. When something is changing, metrics give us the ability to measure that change. In my Gentle Pressure Relentlessly Applied model, the *metrics provide assurance that we are making progress*. That's why the associated outcome is transparency. We want the results to be easily identified. We want there to be no room for interpretation.

The transparency (visibility) that metrics offer will give you many additional benefits:

- Your team can see through the improving metrics that their efforts are working. This provides inspiration, increasing commitment, and momentum.
- You can identify quickly that your approach is the right one, validating the process for future use and training.
- You can also see if the approach needs correcting. If you're getting no results, perhaps you should reconsider your approach—making changes in time to still achieve your desired results.
- You reduce the possibility of emotionally-based interpretation. The results speak for themselves.
- You build trust when your team knows that decisions are made based on ongoing, measurable results—not whims. This trust trickles into other areas of leadership. As David Horsager, author of *The Trust Edge*, states, "Whether you are a student or a CEO, a teacher or a parent, a politician or a nurse, trust multiples influence and impact" (Horsager 2009, 8).

Look at examples from this in everyday life:

- You child complains of a headache. You grab a thermometer and take her temperature. It's not that you doubt your child's story, but the metrics (temperature) give you visibility into what had previously been a child's perception. A temperature of

99.9 with no other symptoms gets a vastly different response than a temperature of 103, coughing, and nausea. Continuing to check her temperature lets you know (assures you) that the treatment is making progress (as the temperature is reduced), or that additional methods of treatment are needed to achieve a favorable result.

- You invest your money in a company's stock. You've researched the company and like their direction. You believe they're going to grow and that by investing in them, you stand to make a profit. The stock market marches on, and you occasionally monitor the overall performance by looking at your financial results. These are expressed as percentages as well as dollar amounts. Regardless of your research, your opinion, or your confidence, only these metrics assure you a result.

Two years ago, after an extended period of business travel, I noticed a significant weight gain. I'd gone to see my family doctor because of some inner-ear pain and found that I'd put on twenty-five pounds of unpleasant (right-on-my-midsection) weight. My son, Kent—somewhat of a nutrition expert—correctly identified that I wasn't only sedentary, but I was also eating badly. I had to make a choice for my health.

He put me on a keto diet. If you're not familiar with keto, the approach drastically reduces your carbohydrate intake. You know, potatoes, most fruits, most processed foods, breads, sugars, grains, pasta…basically anything good is off limits. No more sugar in my coffee, no more snacks with movies, no more happy hour.

Remembering my goal, I set out to change my life. I was disciplined, determined, and made the abrupt, difficult changes. Weekly, at the exact same time, I checked my weight (my Metric for Assurance). If I was going to rid myself of all the good foods, I certainly wanted assurance it was working. For me, it did work! Within two and a half months, I'd lost the target weight, increased my exercise regimen, and felt accomplished and healthier as a result.

On the flip side, consider what happens when Metrics for Assurance are absent—or lost. John Kennedy Jr. died in a tragic airplane crash on July 16, 1999. He was the pilot. He had his wife and sister-in-law in the plane with him. Certainly, he was fully motivated to fly safely and protect his—and their—lives. Yet he had only three hundred hours of flying experience and was not instrument rated—which meant he was not licensed to fly a plane using only instruments, without sight.

As he flew, it was a hazy night with no moon. After the crash, the investigation concluded there were no mechanical issues, and based on his plane's flight path, he'd made no abrupt changes in flight. He simply lost visual sight of the horizon and was unable to see lights or landmarks. His inability to confirm his location or flight path by using metrics—in the form of instrumentation, dials, etc.—and his lack of training (which we will discuss soon!), meant that he flew his plane straight into the ocean without any alarm along the way (Logistics Online 2022).

This tragedy reminds us of the risk when we don't assign metrics to the behaviors we want to change.

Notice here that Metrics for Assurance is supported by the theme of *pressure*. The metrics form the pressure needed to create change. Once a number is attached to an effort, for example, there is immediate—and growing—pressure. Consider these examples:

- How many nights have you set an alarm in order to wake up in time to make an early morning flight? When I do, I often have trouble sleeping out of a fear of the alarm not going off, causing me to miss the flight. I toss and turn, thinking: *Did I set the time to a.m. or p.m.? Is the volume setting loud enough to wake me up? Have I allowed enough time to get to the airport?* Pressure.
- What if you were a high school senior who dreamt of attending Harvard University? In addition to your high school extracurricular career and GPA score, you would need a good SAT score to gain admission. A quick bit of research reveals that you would need an SAT combined score of 1580 to give yourself the best chance to be considered. As you sit down to start the grueling test, you can see that number flashing in your head: *1580...1580...1580.* Pressure.

- Let's say your team just implemented a new online system to allow customers more access to their own data, as well as to solutions and answers to common problems. To measure whether the new platform works, you set up metrics to measure customer satisfaction, numbers of complaints lodged to customer service, and overall staff time spent managing these problems. Over time, you watch these numbers to see if the change is working. Pressure.

Here's the thing: if pressure isn't created by the metrics you chose, then the pressure for results will have to come from you, the leader. You will be constantly circling back to remind your team of their responsibility. You will have to manufacture some sort of punishment/reward system to keep people moving forward. You will find yourself feeling all the pressure for results—and your team will feel none of it. Or worse yet, you will have no idea if your change is effective, and confidence and trust will plummet.

Creating this pressure—through metrics—is the key to ultimately developing and enjoying a Culture of Accountability.

SKILLS

This section addresses the inevitable need to develop—through the Training and Coaching phase—the *skills* needed to accomplish the task at hand. If you want your team to win at basketball, they will need to develop dribbling, passing, and shooting skills. If you want to have a successful sales team, you must develop communication, persuasion, and rapport-building skills. If you want to win a political office, you must develop the skills of public speaking, fundraising, and all the powers of persuasion you can assemble.

That's why this phase is called Training and Coaching. Let's explore the distinction, which we will detail more in chapter 7.

- *Training* refers to the activities (often delivered in a group setting) offered by an organization to transfer the critical knowledge, skills, techniques, etc. to team members, so they can successfully engage in the required tasks (such as those needed in a change process).
- *Coaching* involves reinforcement (typically one-on-one by a leader or mentor) of the necessary behaviors to develop a team member's skills—not just for some future use, but for the here and now.

Both are needed, and each requires a unique skill set to administer. Think of young athletes going to a workshop on how to play more effective soccer. They receive group training through short lectures and demonstrations. Then they practice their new skills and techniques. As they demonstrate what they've learned, coaching comes into play as the instructor or coach gives them individualized direction on how to adjust their actions. "Follow through more on that next kick to get more power," the coach might say.

In a business setting, you may conduct training on a specific set of skills, but the coaching is what allows a leader or expert to reinforce the training in action. Think of customer service training, where a group is given an overview on a new approach and script. Then the first live call comes in, and the customer service agent implements the change. A coach then sits with the agent after the call to go over what they did correct, as well as what they can change for the next time. This process reinforces the new "right" way of operating.

If you intend to lead change, you can expect that you'll need a significant commitment to training and coaching. But don't panic and think you must do all of this on your own. It's common and advisable to bring in outsiders at times to train on areas that need specialized expertise. For example, if you're implementing a major software change, such as to your enterprise resource planning (ERP) system, you may bring in technology experts. These trainers can guide your subject matter experts and business leads in using the new system, while planning for any necessary modifications based on your organization's unique needs. You may even want to bring in an outside trainer to deliver change management sessions. Doing so can equip your leaders or managers to guide people through the emotional side of change—developing the interpersonal skills to thrive through change.

We will discuss Training and Coaching in much more depth in its later chapter once we dive fully into implementing the phases.

INTEGRITY

Look at the infographic for Gentle Pressure Relentlessly Applied again. For the Applied component, if you view the graphic vertically, you see the Culture of Accountability phase—which is fueled by a theme of Integrity.

A Culture of Accountability is one where your team members act intentionally to serve your overall organizational goals, as well as to engage one another. They hold themselves and each other accountable, and your systems reinforce the most important Metrics for Assurance.

The Importance of Follow-Up

One element is key in creating a Culture of Accountability: follow-up. Ultimately, if you intend to create a Culture of Accountability, you must have follow-up. Following up is the actual *test* of your integrity. In other words, *you do what you say you will do.*

For example, I've managed—and trained—many sales teams. Over the years, I've learned that the greatest failure in sales performance is the lack of follow-up. So many salespeople have earned a poor reputation (as unreliable, self-centered, competitive, insincere, etc.) because they make promises, then fail to deliver on them.

This breakdown starts in the simplest of ways: "I'll call you tomorrow," but it ends with major disruptions and broken relationships. This is why disciplined salespeople rely on some sort of customer relationship management (CRM) system to help them remember their promises. These technologies create reminders and alarms for follow-up—to reinforce the Culture of Accountability.

My business partner, Leslie, has mastered this approach. Several years ago, she was speaking with a prospect about signing up for one of our programs. After forty-five minutes of a conversation, the prospect said, "Thanks for your time today, but the timing just isn't right."

She then asked, "So when do you think the best timing would be for you to reconsider this?"

"Give me six months," he replied.

Six months happened to be March 5. So Leslie set herself a reminder to call him on March 5 and went about the rest of her day.

Six months later, on March 5, the reminder showed up on Leslie's calendar. She picked up the phone and said, "I'm calling six months later as promised!"

The prospect laughed out loud and said, "I remember you calling! I can't believe you actually followed up. How do I sign up?"

Guess what? This guy is still a client today.

Where Does Integrity Come In?

Usually when we read the word *integrity*, we think of honesty. Look a little deeper. The origin of the word is Latin, *Integer*. It means, simply, "whole" or "complete."

For our purpose, Integrity means that you will leave nothing undone in your process of Gentle Pressure Relentlessly Applied. Integrity is the Application. Integrity begins with doing what you say you will do.

Consider that Gentle, Pressure, and Relentless don't have any impact unless they're Applied. In the context of Gentle Pressure Relentlessly Applied, Integrity is demonstrated in the insistence you exhibit by your follow-up.

Your follow-up isn't always in the form of a sales call. Sometimes it's another step you must take to remain accountable to your desired outcome. *Applied* means that you have initiated the next steps.

- You have asked the hard question.
- You have completed your research.
- You have called the meeting.
- You haven't forgotten what you promised.

Pressure is applied. Integrity is confirmed.

Culture of Accountability: This Is Where the Rubber Meets the Road

There's a great motivational poster I sometimes see in retail running stores. It reads, "If running is difficult, run more." I love it because it's a simple truth: Running is difficult for many of us. If you want it to become easier, just do more of it!

I don't really need to teach you how to set your alarm to get up earlier. I probably don't need to remind you to hydrate for the run. You don't need me to lay out a route for you to run. If you want to make running easier, you just have to decide to run more.

The same is true with Applying Relentless Pressure Gently (yes, I reworded my mantra!). If you want to get results, make changes, and achieve your vision with others, you must have the integrity to consistently do what you say you will do. Follow up. Set the meeting. Establish the standard. Ask the hard question. Follow the process completely. Leave nothing out. Be relentless. Be Gentle. Create Pressure. And you be the one to Apply it.

If Gentle Pressure is difficult to apply, apply it more!

CHAPTER 5

AGREEMENT ON APPROACH

NOW THAT WE'VE explored the structure behind the process and gained a deeper understanding of the desired outcomes it's time to dive into how to implement each of the four phases of the Gentle Pressure Relentlessly Applied process.

The first and most crucial phase is also the most challenging: acquiring an Agreement on Approach. You must make every effort to secure alignment with every member of your team through this agreement, which:

- Creates power in your communication, as you all understand the context of your work, and removes assumptions about the approach;
- Builds alignment, maximizing everyone's efforts in the same direction with unity, increased results, and synergy;
- Results in focus, minimizing distractions and disagreements so that you and your team can redirect energy to the project.

The benefits to securing your Agreement on Approach are clear, as are the downfalls if you skip this phase. Fortunately for you, this chapter shows you just how to do it—exploring pitfalls as well as specific tactics to make it happen. Onward and upward!

ASSUMED BUY-IN IS YOUR FIRST MISTAKE

The most common mistake I see among leaders and managers is believing that all team members agree with their approach. These leaders are moving confidently in the direction they believe is best—without looking back to see whether others are engaged. Some team members may actually be pulling in the opposite direction! The time to address this is *not* when your project is underway. The time to address this is before you start.

Picture this: you're coaching a Little League baseball team. As the coach, you've decided that the highest priority for you (your approach) is to teach the game to all players and give each equal playing time.

However, you mistakenly believe that all parents of the team members will agree with this approach and support it. Three games into the season, a small group of parents confront you after a game because they're "tired of losing." In fact, they go so far as to say, "You're embarrassing us!"

This is the result of failure to secure an Agreement on Approach—with all parents, from the beginning. In this case, your Agreement on Approach would have stated that allowing every player time on the field is priority—along with sportsmanship. Winning, while something that is inherently a desirable goal in sports, would not be part of your Agreement on Approach.

Many youth sports leagues now go as far as requiring parents to watch a video and sign such an agreement to head off unsportsmanlike behavior—from the parents! Even if it may seem annoying to a busy parent to watch a video on how *not* to yell at the coach (or players!), these teams are doing something right.

This type of misalignment happens all the time. Problems occur because we don't secure an Agreement on Approach. But how do you achieve it? Let's explore.

We will explore some examples and break them down into how and where the misalignment occurs. For each of the following examples, note how each person has a different approach.

- **Hiring a salesperson on a commission compensation plan.**
    - Your approach is to create a customer-centric service experience with a team of motivated professionals.
    - The salesperson's approach is to increase her salary by aggressively working with as many customers as possible, even if that makes customers uncomfortable and offends the rest of the team.
- **Planning a vacation with another family.**
    - Your approach is to find a new part of the country where you've never been. Once there, you will explore all the sites, discover new culinary experiences, learn some history, and enjoy gaining some new perspectives.
    - Your friend's approach is to find a relaxing locale with comfy furniture for slowing down—bringing the kids along, and letting them swim and play together to burn off steam. *This may be a good time to catch up on some overdue reading,* your friend thinks.

- **Promoting your most productive team member to management.**
    - Your approach is to continue enjoying all of her great production while leveraging her insights and approach with others on the team. She'll be teaching everyone on the team her techniques, and you'll enjoy another 50 percent growth in the department.
    - Her approach is to finally enjoy the fruits of all her labor. She's worked hard. Now it's time to manage the team from the safety of her office. Settling into her new life in middle management, she's asking herself: *how do I take my coffee?!*

As you can see from the examples, alignment doesn't occur automatically. In fact, it's so easy to have misalignment. When this happens, it's because you haven't secured buy-in from each person on your team. You may assume you have buy-in, but unless you've gone through the phase of securing Agreement on Approach, you aren't there yet.

Once you understand human nature, you can clearly see the fallacy of assumed buy-in. People have a quirky tendency to want to do things their own way. I see this tendency even if it's clear that "their way" isn't going to work. That's why, if you're leading change, you can't take this step for granted. The word *assume* should be a clue. It's defined as, "to believe something without evidence." The original Latin means, "to take." So when you assume, you have taken a belief without any evidence. This is not a good first step if you want to lead change.

Leaders and managers who merely send out emails and memos or display messages via Post-It notes on a bulletin board often find themselves surprised that people aren't doing what they request.

- "I addressed this at last week's staff meeting!"
- "We've sent at least ten emails about this. Why aren't people responding?"
- "I'll attach a note on their monitor. Let's see them ignore that!"

This can even breed animosity, as leaders feel they're being willfully ignored, even as employees feel they haven't been properly informed. Without an Agreement on Approach, this is all too common!

At first glance, it may appear that I don't trust people. This isn't true. In fact, I can cite numerous examples where I've gone overboard to support people despite the fact that they had already taken advantage of me. I believe one of the most useful attributes of a leader is to believe the best in the people on their team. Even when you do this, however, you can't assume that people have bought in to your Approach just because you announced it.

You only invite aggravation and delay when you skip the phase of getting Agreement on Approach. Despite the challenges inherent in this phase, commit now to do it, no matter the obstacles.

Just this week, I was celebrating my birthday over a bourbon with my good friend, Trevor. We were talking about his job. He's a regional sales rep for an organization that sells aftermarket parts for motorcycles. He'd recently been called to the corporate office, where the national sales manager announced a new program for improving sales. All of the regional sales reps were present (more than thirty). The national sales manager thought he'd done his homework and had a beautiful presentation.

As Trevor was telling me his story, however, he shared with me what he was thinking as the presentation was happening:

- *This won't work.*
- *I've seen this sort of thing before. My accounts won't go for it.*
- *There's a simpler, more effective way we should consider.*
- *They've already invested too much money in this program for me to change their minds, so I'm just going to keep quiet.*

Trevor looked at me, cut his eyes to the side, and said, "I'm not going to spend any time on it."

I could tell. He wasn't going to change his approach. His manager hadn't changed his mind. He would continue on his previous approach. No change.

Just look at all the lost opportunity in this exchange:

- Trevor isn't going to spend any time on the sales manager's new program.

- Trevor is likely to reduce his collaboration with the sales manager in future sales promotions.
- The sales manager doesn't know anything about Trevor's alternative options.
- Their relationship isn't strengthened.

...and most of all,

- The sales manager believes everyone is onboard and assumes all sales reps will be implementing the new program—but Trevor "isn't going to spend any time on it."
- The sales manager can't rely on his savvy PowerPoint to convince his team. Nor can the sales manager count on the weight of a large group meeting to add value to the new program.

If there's any advice I'd give you to dramatically increase your leadership skills, it's this: DON'T ASSUME YOUR TEAM HAS BOUGHT IN TO YOUR PLAN, JUST BECAUSE YOU HELD A MEETING. We've all made the mistake of assumption. Assuming your team is onboard without confirming will stop your change momentum in its tracks.

HOW TO SECURE AN AGREEMENT ON APPROACH

The following four subsections of this chapter (Dialogue, One on One, Human Nature, and Enrollment) are the necessary steps to achieving buy-in through your Agreement on Approach. Remember, in this first phase of Gentle Pressure Relentlessly Applied, it's your absolute priority to ensure that you have achieved this Agreement on Approach. You can't skip this step. You can't assume that your team members see things from the same perspective as you.

Therefore, if no one else is formally in the role to do so, *you* take the initiative. *You* call the meeting. *You* create the approach you want. *You* plan a compelling way to explain and convince others on your team that this approach is the best way. And even if someone else is formally sponsoring the initiative, you can still be a champion for making this happen. Share the Gentle Pressure Relentlessly Applied process with them, and ask them for cooperation in seeking an Agreement on Approach.

Even with a meeting set or support from a sponsor, this process won't always be simple. In fact, it usually isn't. In my book, *ORBiT*, I have a chapter titled, "Change Requires a Compelling Reason Why." If you're expecting people to change their approach to something, you'll have to be compelling in your reasoning. Asking people to change anything will require a superhuman effort on your part (Mann 2017). Remember, human nature is to resist change! Consider this quote:

> *"Progress is a nice word. But change is its motivator. And change has its enemies."*
>
> —Robert Kennedy

One of the greatest enemies of change is—get ready for this—ineffective leadership. What should you do to be effective? Read ahead!

Dialogue in a Safe Environment

So, let's create the result we want, shall we? The first step to achieving Agreement on Approach when leading change is to *create an open dialogue in a safe environment.*

Dialogue is an important word. When we do strategic planning with our clients, we start with some definitions. Of particular importance is the group's understanding of the difference between *discussion* and *dialogue.*

- **We use *discussion* to define the types of conversations which are intended to result in decisions.** In discussions, we weigh the merits of various ideas, edit some options, and come to agreement on the way forward.
- **We use *dialogue* to define the free-flowing exchange of possibilities, even if they don't result in an immediate decision.** In this type of conversation, both parties are equal participants. Ideas are welcome. Creativity is encouraged. Possibilities are the goal. Think of it like brainstorming.

The best way to create an Agreement on Approach is through dialogue. That is, from the beginning, all participants are involved in creating the result.

As a strong leader, you may feel it's your responsibility to bring all the answers. However, if you want to build a strong, engaged team of competent achievers, you'll have to give them the opportunity to co-create the approach.

This may seem risky to some. But the alternative is a dictatorship, which will be characterized by rapid turnover, grumbling, high drama (or passive-aggression), and limited results. At first glance, something resembling a dictatorship may seem easier and quicker. In the long run, with achievement-minded individuals, the best approach is dialogue in a safe environment.

What is a *safe environment*? I'm not talking about safety from attack or injury. Rather, I'm describing an ongoing commitment—created by you—to having conversations where ideas can be expressed without judgement, interruption, or dismissal. This is an environment where achievers thrive, where leaders listen and learn, and where the leader's body language communicates openness and receptivity.

In 2012, Google engaged in Project Aristotle to uncover what made their teams most effective. After analyzing the data collected from studying 180 of their teams in action—including conducting more than 200 interviews and analyzing over 250 team attributes—they credited one feature with producing the most successful teams. Those teams didn't necessarily have the best planning or the most deep and diverse skills. Rather, they established *psychological safety* (Google 2022).

That is, members felt safe taking risks by speaking up about their ideas. They felt listened to, respected, and like their opinions mattered. They were willing to be vulnerable when contributing ideas to the team, lacking fear that they might be ridiculed or viewed as incompetent.

Harvard Business School professor Amy Edmondson defined psychological safety in a 1999 report as a "shared belief held by members of a team that the team is safe for interpersonal risk-taking." She said that psychological safety is "a sense of confidence that the team will not embarrass, reject, or punish someone for speaking up…It describes a team climate characterized by interpersonal trust and mutual respect in which people are comfortable being themselves." (Edmondson 1999, 350-83).

A safe environment for dialogue takes time, patience, self-discipline, and practice. This isn't effective if you only create a safe environment when you want something from your team. This safe environment must be a "way of being" for you, not a technique that is used to manipulate to a predetermined end result.

Start by creating a welcome environment for dialogue all the time, and you'll find it highly effective when you intend to lead change. Here are the elements of a safe environment for dialogue that you as a leader should implement:

- Don't tolerate interrupting; let the speaker finish.
- Stay focused, with no multitasking.
- Remain un-rushed.
- Ask questions for clarification.
- Realize that when you make someone wrong, you lose.

- You lose the chance to possibly learn something. You lose the chance to deepen the relationship. You lose a little trust in the relationship. You lose the opportunity to influence.

In fairness, you should set some standards for the people who join you in this safe environment. For example, they should agree to *work by proxy*. That is, anyone who comes to the conversation with their own agenda ("axe to grind") won't be an equal participant. They must understand that their participation is by proxy. This means that your colleague is representing other current and future members of your team. Decisions therefore must be made for the good of the group, not for any one individual. When a colleague can't agree to this, you don't have a safe environment.

One of the most influential books of the twentieth century was the bestselling *Seven Habits of Highly Effective People* by Steven Covey. Covey made famous the phrase, "think win/win" as his fourth habit of the seven. But this habit is often oversimplified. He introduces "six paradigms of human interaction," with "win/win" sometimes being tied to "no deal."

No deal!? Yes, the commitment is to find a win-win, or to walk away with no hard feelings. As Covey states, "No Deal basically means that if we can't find a solution that would benefit us both, we agree to disagree agreeably—No Deal" (Covey 1994).

This may feel risky, but can you imagine an open, transparent relationship—even with your subordinates—where you are committed to a win-win relationship? From the perspective of your team, those you want to influence, they now have a receptive vessel. You are open, transparent, and truly able to listen. You've created a truly safe environment for people to collaborate, dialogue, share ideas, and be part of the solution.

But remember, you also hold in reserve the right to find "no deal."

Too many leaders approach meetings with an agenda of items they must get others to agree to as-is. This myopic approach is easy to see through and eventually erodes trust and open dialogue. The better path is to commit to a discussion/dialogue where the mutual agreement is to find a win-win *or no deal*. This places the risk equally on both parties. If you can't find a win-win, agree to shake hands and walk away.

Back in the early nineties, I was managing my first retail store in Memphis, Tennessee. The company had a strict policy requiring all sales staff to wear only clothing that was sold in the store. One of my salespeople (who happened to be one of the top producers) suddenly became disenchanted with this policy and began to wear outfits outside of the dress code. After a few "write-ups," I sat down with him to explore some options. I told him I'd like to find a win-win. The "win" for me, of course, was that he would follow company policy.

The challenge was that I needed a safe environment for him to express his views, opinions, and ideas. So, we scheduled a time to dialogue about the company policy.

Unfortunately, he didn't want to dialogue. He came to the meeting with a series of *fogging* techniques: "I'm your number one salesperson," "I shouldn't have to be held to this standard," "Clearly this is working for me," etc.

At the end of the dialogue, unfortunately, we didn't have a win-win. We looked at each other and calmly agreed: *we can't work together*. He went his way, and Bachrach Memphis went on to enjoy a 35 percent increase in sales revenue for the season.

Do This One-on-One

In the interest of leading change, attempting to secure Agreement on Approach via a group effort is likely the single biggest mistake leaders make. Consider which of these are the least effective methods of business communication:

- Email
- Memos
- Voicemail
- Announcements made in group meetings

Look at this list again. You can say that all of these channels have a purpose, but they also all come with shortcomings. You also can attest that these are the *most used* methods of business communication. Many of us send out an email announcing a new plan, process, or directive, and without follow-up or dialogue, we assume that the message has been heard, read, understood, agreed to, and that the recipient is well on their way to implementation. As we discussed earlier in this chapter, if only it were that easy.

Why do we most often choose these less than effective methods? In my work, I've observed that it happens because we believe there's just no time to approach people one-on-one. Instead, we broadcast the directive and let the chips fall where they may. "At least I've done my job," we say, shrugging our shoulders when an employee literally or figuratively "doesn't get the memo."

In some cases, leaders choose these ineffective methods because they *don't* want to engage in a dialogue. They want their directives read and implemented without conversation or input (Gallup 1999). Unfortunately, we've all probably worked for this kind of boss.

While I am not advocating scrapping all other means of group communication, I'm suggesting that they can't exist in isolation from one-on-one conversations. These dialogues are what engage each person in your change.

Much has been said and done about *employee engagement* in the workplace. Gallup publishes regular results on the state of engagement in the US, as well as the high monetary cost of disengagement—$60.3 million, as reported in 2020 (Herway 2020). What then is engagement? "Engagement refers to the level of dedication, commitment, passion, innovation, and emotional energy a person is willing to expend. An engaged employee gives of their discretionary effort," states Scott Carbonara, author of *Manager's Guide to Employee Engagement* (Carbonara 2013).

Gallup also studies engagement in the context of its "Q12"—that is, twelve statements for employees which, when answered positively (with a five out of five answer), signify high engagement. Each of these statements ties to an employee need, which is directly correlated to engagement. Would it surprise you to learn that one of those statements is: "At work, my opinions seem to count"?

So why do I recommend that you have the Agreement on Approach conversation one-on-one? *Because it counts the opinions of each individual, thereby engaging team members in the process of change. That's the only way to ensure the outcome of alignment.* And having an aligned team is the only way to effectively get the results you want when you're leading change.

One-on-one conversations allow for feedback. They allow for discovery. They allow all the emotional responses to be uncovered and addressed. Resistance can be resolved, and relationships can be enriched. If I had to sum this up, I'd say: *I like them, because they work.*

This one-on-one approach exposes a key attribute you must have as a leader: listening. In your one-on-one session, you are either:

- Committed to listening to the other person, or
- Trying to intimidate and insist on your will.

In the context of securing an Agreement on Approach, there is only one effective way: *you must be committed to listening.* Listening is the strongest and often most overlooked communication skill. The key to effective leadership lies in effective communication, and the key to effective communication lies in genuine listening. By listening with attention and comprehension, you show empathy—a key leadership trait we mentioned earlier in the book. This highlights emotional intelligence and allows you to influence with integrity while still building relationships.

We all like to believe we're effective listeners, but the truth is that few of us are. In fact, our brains seem to be predisposed to work against effective listening. Think about this: how many words per minute can you speak? In normal conversation, you're probably only speaking sixty words or so a minute (plus a few pauses)(Gutoskey 2022). How quickly do you read? Most people read between 250 to 400 words per minute. Speed-readers can exceed 700 words per minute. Now, try to calculate how many words, thoughts, images, and impulses your mind can think of in one minute. It's difficult to imagine. So, here you are attempting to listen to someone talk who is speaking sixty words per minute, while your brain is capable of hearing, processing, and responding to thousands of images, words, and ideas in a single minute.

You see? Your brain is working so much faster than the person who is talking. Because of this, it's not uncommon to get distracted or bored when someone is talking to us. Because of this reality, we've developed a series of bad habits which become barriers to our listening effectiveness.

Following are the habits I see causing the most problems, some of which we hinted at in the step on creating an environment of safety.

Interrupting. To see this demonstrated, all you have to do is sit on the sidelines of your next social event and watch others' conversations. It may be amazing to watch the back and forth of people habitually interrupting each other. I've often wondered, since this is such an obvious communication flaw, why do people do it?

- Sometimes people are simply caught up in the conversation, excited by what they've heard, and the interruption is just a reaction. ("I loved that movie. We just watched it last night!")
- Other times, I see people trying to create connection and rapport, so they immediately respond when they have something to add—which connects us to the person we're speaking to. ("We were there on vacation two years ago—one of my favorite places!")
- I've watched many well-meaning people interrupt, just because they have a point to make and don't want to forget it.

As well-meaning as these reasons may be, the net effect in all cases is that someone was interrupted while speaking.

Assumption/Interpreting. This is a common habit, especially when we know the person we're speaking to well. This happens in personal and business relationships all the time. You've been together for years. You know their tendencies. You've heard all of their stories. You've had the same disagreements numerous times. As soon as a hot topic is introduced and they start a predictable response or story, you find yourself rolling your eyes and having the same emotional reaction you did the last time they told this story. Assumptions don't serve us well, because once you make them you have stopped listening.

Multitasking. This is probably the primary culprit to preventing effective listening. When you're trying to do multiple things at once, you're usually not doing one of them (or any of them) very well. In fact, this is backed by research. A 2006 report by the American Psychological Association states, "Psychologists who study what happens to cognition (mental processes) when people try to perform more than one task at a time have found that the mind and brain were not designed for heavy-duty multitasking" (APA 2006). This scientific fact is the reason why the Department of Transportation doesn't allow you to text and drive. Your driving isn't safe, and your texts are misspelled! Of course, you can probably remember times when someone was talking to you while you were reading or checking something on your phone. You knew they were speaking, but you had no recollection of what they'd said. "I'm sorry, could you repeat that?" you responded. Putting away your phone, laptop, or any reading materials is the first step to effective listening. In fact, research shows that much of communication happens through body language and other non-verbal actions.

But there's another, more insidious type of multi-tasking. It's the common habit of self-talk that goes on internally when someone else is talking. That self-dialogue literally prevents us from hearing what the other person says.

It looks like this:

- **You, meeting someone for the first time:** "Hi, my name is Dan, how are you?"
- **Judy, shaking your hand:** "Hi Dan, my name is Judy, nice to meet you! Where are you from?"
- **You, internally thinking to yourself while she is speaking:** "I like her briefcase; I must be sure to ask about it later."

Because of this conflicting, multitasking, internal conversation, you didn't hear what Judy said. Even though she just told you her name, you didn't "hear" it, so now you progress through the conversation, desperately trying to figure out a way to learn it without asking again!

If this seems familiar to you, multitasking has become a listening obstacle.

To avoid all these habits, consider these tactics to improve your listening:

- **Maintain open, approachable body language.** Don't "cross" anything. Keep your shoulders square, facing the speaker.
- **Picture what's being said.** Imagine it, and don't let your mind drift.
- **No need to offer solutions; listen to discover.**

- **Be curious.** Your questions are to clarify and ensure understanding.
- **Slow your brain.** Focus and be aware of your tendency to listen faster than the speaker can speak.

The point of a one-on-one conversation when gaining Agreement on Approach is to open the lines of communication, build trust, understand, and *then, to be understood.* Make sure no bad habits creep into this meeting that could undermine your best efforts. A one-on-one meeting represents that this person is valued, important to the cause, and has something to contribute. Make sure that's your intent.

Understand Human Nature

As we go through the first phase in the Gentle Pressure Relentlessly Applied process, gaining Agreement on Approach, that first word is likely your first and biggest obstacle to success: *agreement.* It seems so easy! *Why can't everyone just see it like I do? Why don't they "get it"? Why is she so stubborn? Why is he so set in his ways?*

The answer lies in *human nature.*

That's right, we're built this way. For some reason, we humans have this peculiar ability to form an opinion based on our experiences, and then take a lifetime to confirm and reconfirm that opinion with everything we read, observe, and encounter. (Read more about this in the Metrics for Assurance chapter, where we discuss *confirmation bias.*) Many of these patterns exist without our awareness, which is why they can lead to *unconscious bias.*

We're all guilty of forming a mindset and sticking with it, often to our very detriment. Look again at the word more carefully: *Mind. Set.* Your mind is set, finished, done, complete, made up. On the face of it, what a sad position to be in. Nothing else to learn. No new information to absorb. Complete.

Here's the way a mindset is formed.

1. It begins with a *thought*.
2. Thoughts always translate into *actions*.
3. Our actions naturally bring about *results*.
4. Those results then confirm what we thought to begin with, and now they become our *beliefs*.

There you have it—a mindset.

I'll share a dangerous mindset I've often developed: *The city I live in (Asheville, North Carolina) is filled with terrible and rude drivers.* If those are my thoughts when I leave my house in my car, just look at this mindset in action:

- **Thought:** *Asheville drivers are unskilled and rude.*
- **Action:** I drive aggressively to protect myself from them.
- **Result:** My quick turns and tense body language invite a similar behavior from another driver, who moves to cut me off and glare at me as he does.
- **Belief:** *See there? Every time I go out it's the same thing—rude, outrageous drivers.*

Here's the simple way to reset that mindset. Start with a different thought, and discipline yourself to stay out of the old mindset:

- **Thought:** *Asheville is a beautiful place to live, where drivers are often distracted by spectacular views.*
- **Action:** I observe the driver ahead of me failing to allow me to merge.
- **Result:** I smile as I also see the mountains in the distance and think to myself: *No wonder he didn't let me in. He was distracted by that view and never saw me.*
- **Belief:** *This certainly is a great place to enjoy nature's beauty.*

You may be laughing at this example—especially if you (like me) struggle with the drivers in your town! But think about the impact on your stress levels and mood if you engaged your mindset to see your experiences differently. Instead of, *that arrogant driver just intentionally and carelessly cut in front of me*, your thought could be, *that driver is headed home in a hurry to respond to a family emergency.*

That little mindset change can make a huge difference in the way you feel for the rest of your day. Instead of stress, you're more relaxed. Instead of responding with dangerous, aggressive driving, you're remaining calm, aware, and safe. All because of your mindset change.

So, let's take this awareness of human nature and apply it to the situations where you must secure Agreement on Approach. Do you see how the mindsets of others are your primary obstacle? The business of convincing someone else to change their beliefs is challenging—and seemingly impossible. There's a reason most of us stay away from the topics of religion and politics when engaging in polite conversation. As I look at my social media feed and see friends and family "preach to the choir" about their dearly-held views, I often wonder who they think they're converting.

If you didn't grow up going to church (as I did), you may not understand this metaphor, "preaching to the choir." Picture it: Sunday morning. The pastor begins preaching. At the back of the stage sits the choir. These are the most committed, most fervent of the congregation. If the pastor wants to be reinforced in the message of the day, all he must do is turn around, face the choir, and raise his voice. There, based on the choir's fervent response, the pastor can receive all the passionate support he needs to confirm the message of the day—preaching to the choir.

When you expect to tackle the current mindset of a team member who isn't in alignment with your approach, remember that people have all sorts of tactics and methods to maintain their dearly-held beliefs. *MIND. SET.*

So let me remind you here, you probably *can't* change someone's mindset. The reality of human nature dictates that people must change their mindset *on their own*. That's why I call this next step *enrollment*. Changing a mindset involves a choice: theirs.

Enrollment

Let's remember this vital point: if you're asking your team to agree on your approach, and you want to absolutely ensure alignment, your team members must voluntarily agree.

I use the word *enrollment* intentionally here. The mental image I have is the process someone goes through to choose a college. When students graduate from high school, they have so many choices: in-state, out-of-state, public, private, and the list goes on. Would the student choose the school based on the perceived quality of education? Would the choice be based on the football team's record? Would the choice be based on family history? Some other basis?

However the choice is made, eventually the student chooses. Applications are submitted. Pre-enrollment requirements are finalized. Paperwork is signed. Deposits are sent, and promises made. The student has made a choice and has *enrolled*.

In the course of your leadership, remember your need to provide the context, inspiration, rationale, and basis for why your team members should enroll to your approach. You want to portray that:

- Your "cause" is worthy.
- The approach has been researched and is the correct one.
- The results will be a win-win for all who are involved.
- Accomplishing your quest together will be fulfilling.
- The results will be worth the sacrifice.

Maybe you're thinking, *all I want my team to do is pick up after themselves in the breakroom!*

Fair enough. But let me ask you to consider: if you have a group of adults working for you right now, and you can't get them to own the most reasonable of maintenance tasks, is it possible they don't see the "vision" for a clean breakroom? Is it that they don't see the win-win for the team, or themselves? Can they not yet embrace the personal sacrifice, because they don't know the results will be worth it?

When I teach this in-person, I often get asked, "How can we approach this conversation without being condescending?" Good question. Let's explore it—but before we do, let's look at the reality of a dirty, poorly-maintained breakroom. In this situation:

- We've collectively increased the risk of pests and unsanitary conditions, making it unpleasant to eat future meals in this dedicated space.
- We've selfishly expected that someone else—perhaps someone with a more severe case of OCD—will take up the slack.
- We've set the (low) standard for teamwork and community.

Whatever ends up happening with the breakroom clean-up, there is now a new, dysfunctional approach to addressing a breakdown. So, while it may seem patronizing to bring up these things, failure to do so simply creates disfunction, dissatisfaction, and in this case, an ongoing declining standard.

Just a few pages ago, I stated that humans tend to establish certain mindsets and beliefs, and it's virtually impossible to change those beliefs from the outside; people will make their own choice to change their mindset. That is why securing an Agreement on Approach requires enrollment. Enrolling in something is signing up, enlisting, volunteering, joining. Your job, then, is to create the environment where that is a possibility and a reasonable option.

Here's a simple outline to follow when you want to give someone the option to enroll in an approach. You can add details based on your situation to customize it further.

1. Introduce yourself and tell the person why you chose to meet with them.
2. Ask, "What does it mean to you to have a vision? What is a vision?"
3. Ask, "What is your vision?"
4. Ask, "What is the new future we're trying to create?"
5. Ask, "What will it be like if we can reach that future?"
6. Ask, "What would it be like if you missed out because you chose not to enroll?"
7. Offer an invitation.

Let's apply this outline to the situation of everyone working to keep the breakroom clean. And imagine this not as a speech, but as a dialogue.

1. "Hi, Randy. Thanks for sitting down with me. I've grown concerned about the general maintenance and cleanliness of our breakroom, and I'd like for us to discuss this together."
2. "Do you know what it means to have a vision? Why are visions important?"

3. "Do you remember our company vision?" (Let's use IKEA's, "to create a better everyday life for the many people.")
4. "What do you think this vision has to do with a clean, well-maintained breakroom?"
5. "Picture what a consistently clean breakroom could do for morale, motivation, and an overall better everyday life..."
6. "Can you talk about what our work-life would be like if we didn't make this a priority?"
7. "What do you think? Should we commit together to this new future?"

While this may look condescending as you read it, the goal here is to create a dialogue in a safe environment to give this team member an opportunity to change a mindset and embrace change. The alternatives are to avoid the topic, or worse, to take a passive-aggressive approach of sarcasm and guilt. That's no fun—and it doesn't work.

Closing this enrollment approach may seem like it would take a long time. I would counter with, how much time have you already spent *not* getting results and continuing to be frustrated and ineffective? Invest the time at the outset to secure team enrollment, and you'll be off on the right foot: creating an aligned team with Agreement on Approach.

That's all good—as long as you've selected the right approach!

LESSONS FROM CIRCUIT CITY

In this first phase of Gentle Pressure Relentlessly Applied, gaining Agreement on Approach, I've made the always-dangerous assumption that the Approach you're trying to get agreement on is the right approach. I've learned the hard way that's not always the case. You as the leader must be open to dialogue and input from those you work with. Maybe there's a better way. Maybe you've missed something. Maybe the team is refusing agreement simply because your approach isn't a good one.

In October 2001, the classic business book, *Good To Great*, by Jim Collins was released. In it, he identifies only eleven US companies that were performing at the highest level. There was one retailer in that group. Ever heard of Circuit City? In 2001, Circuit City was the leader in the electronics superstore world. They had hundreds of locations around the US and billions of dollars in sales. It certainly didn't hurt that they were being singled out as one of the eleven best corporations in the country (Collins 2001).

But in March of 2007, CEO Philip Schoonover, motivated by his need to reduce expenses (and perhaps to earn a $7-million bonus), decided to terminate his longest-tenured, most experienced, and highest-paid employees—3,400 of them on the same day (Cohan 2021). He replaced that workforce with 2,100 entry-level, minimum-wage employees. The result should be no surprise. Customer complaints dramatically increased, customer loyalty dramatically decreased, and the tech-hungry public quickly fled to Circuit City's competition,

Best Buy. Circuit City declared bankruptcy less than two years later. Their stores were all closed and the company failed.

Schoonover had a problem he needed to solve. He needed to increase profits and reduce expenses. He made the mistake of choosing cost savings at the expense of great customer service. Prior to this move, Circuit City's legendary expertise and service was its very identity. Their slogan was "Welcome to Circuit City, where service is state of the art."

There's no question that many factors played into Circuit City's demise—rising competition, public interest in all things technology, inflated inventory, etc. There's also no question that the CEO's "approach" to cutting costs directly led to the failure of this one-time industry leader.

I just wonder, what were the conversations like in the offices of their leadership prior to this decision? Did the CEO attempt to secure Agreement on Approach on this terrible idea? Did he look for feedback? Did he really consider all factors? Was there someone who attempted to talk him out of this? Was he listening?

One of the primary reasons I have suggested—

- That you dialogue in a safe place,
- That you have your meetings one-on-one,
- That you consider the influence of human nature,
- That you must allow people to enroll in your approach

—is so that you can hear a conflicting opinion and consider alternatives. This allows you, as the leader, to make the best use of the experience and collaboration of your team.

So if the approach you're seeking agreement on is time-tested, and you're certain of its success, press on. Call the meetings and build alignment. You can operate with all the confidence you need to accomplish the goal.

If, on the other hand, your team members are expressing misgivings, asking you for further investigation, and collectively questioning the approach, maybe it's time for you to review your thinking and revisit the approach.

CHAPTER 6

METRICS FOR ASSURANCE

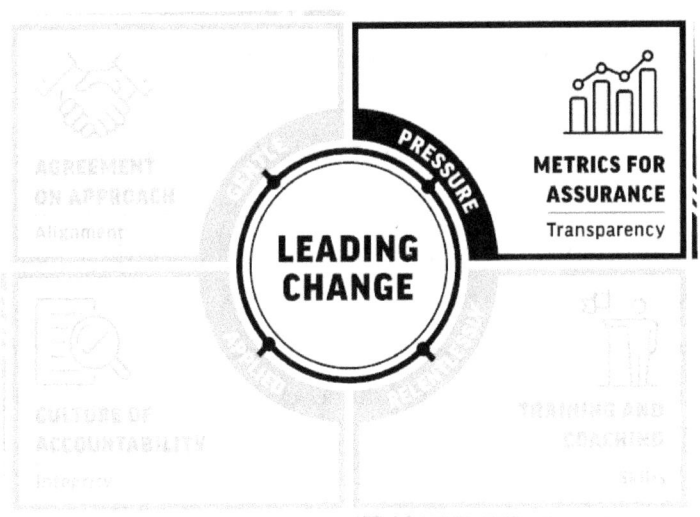

YOU'VE HEARD IT said, "Numbers don't lie." I interpret that to mean that metrics, when used properly, can take the emotion out of your decisions, evaluations, or conclusions.

Well, maybe that's a problem. I've come to understand that each of us has a preferred way we make decisions, gather information, and communicate. Those of us (like me) who are decidedly "right-brained" prefer a more subjective decision-making process. We like to rely on our "gut feeling," trusting our instinct and intuition. We believe that we can make big decisions by navigating what feels right.

In fact, some of us right-brainers actually distrust those who attempt to sway our decisions with numbers. Maybe that's because we don't understand the numbers, or maybe we just don't want to be confused with facts. Perhaps we even think those who decide based on numbers alone are missing some key "stuff" that comes through intuition. Or in some cases, we may have been misled by the use of numbers in a past decision-making process.

Then there's all of you "left-brained" folks. You value accuracy. Objectivity will rule the process. There will be none of this touchy-feely decision-making when you're around. You want to gather all the facts—double-checking those numbers with every type of calculator, abacus, and tape measure available to you. You believe the truth is out there, and with the right spreadsheet we can find it! Over the years, you've likely seen too many leaders make snap judgments and emotion-based decisions, only to see those decisions turn out to be poorly considered and regretted. If only someone had done their homework!

Wherever you land on this spectrum, I would encourage you to move a bit more to the middle. Let's explore why, and how to do it.

The second phase in Gentle Pressure Relentlessly Applied involves incorporating Metrics for Assurance. If you're a "numbers don't lie" fan, then you may land right here in your management formula and never leave. If you're a "numbers may not lie, but liars use numbers" fan, you may wish to avoid this step. In either case, you'll cause your change management process to fall out of balance.

Let's first explore what happens with *too much focus on metrics*. This puts a greater emphasis on "Pressure," which looks something like: Gentle PRESSURE Relentlessly Applied.

Imagine this scenario: your sales manager (focused on metrics) calls her Q2 review meeting. She begins, "Folks, our Q2 revenue was down 34 percent. This, despite the fact that our D2C e-com business is up 93 percent over LY. I know that 5 percent of our locations were closed TY over LY. However, traffic is up 65 percent over the same timeframe, and our conversion rate remained steady at 31 percent. This simply will not stand! As of now, all Q3 PTO is cancelled. We will begin weekly reviews of individual performance on Monday. That's all for now!"

Yikes! Can I buy a vowel? Even if you understand these metrics, gleaning the takeaway message from this communication—especially as it pertains to a change initiative—becomes challenging.

Contrast that with *no focus on metrics*, which looks something like this: GENTLE pressure Relentlessly Applied.

Now picture this management approach applied to the same meeting: "Good morning, everyone. How are you feeling today? I know it's been tough. Our Q2 didn't turn out like we'd hoped. On the bright side, however, some areas of our performance were as good as last year, and our e-com team did really, really well. So, here's what we're going to do. I'm adding forty hours of PTO time to each of you, in order for you to refresh and recover. Starting Monday, I'm also going to be bringing in lunch for all of you, so we can eat together and share our feelings. Have a great weekend!"

Nope. In this situation, you can watch your team—and the company—sink slowly into oblivion. Hey, but at least you are doing it together over lunch!

Instead of either of these scenarios, let's commit to an equal distribution of our four phases within Gentle Pressure Relentlessly Applied. Metrics deserve their place—as long as you're:

- Looking at the right things; and
- Focusing on managing people, not machines.

Remember, without metrics, there will be no transparency—and no pressure.

This is a tough section. For some of you, this will be the most challenging phase of this process. You may be asking these understandable and valid questions:

- "What metrics should I be using?"
- "How do I apply metrics to this unique situation?"
- "Who should be looking at them? How often?"

Or you may not be there yet. You may simply be saying:

- "This will be a big change in how we do things!"

Yes, this will be challenging. Leading change always is. But you need this step to keep yourself—and your team—on the right track. Without the proper application of metrics in your process:

- You will have a difficult time creating accountability.
- You won't know how you're progressing toward your goal.
- You will repeat the same mistakes.
- You will be frustrated by the lack of compliance.

Without Metrics for Assurance, you won't achieve the outcome of *transparency,* as we've discussed. Your team will be in the dark about your true progress, with no milestones or measures of accountability, and your change initiative will falter.

For those who tend to focus exclusively on metrics, the challenge is a bit different. Without the proper context, and when depending too much on numbers:

- You risk alienating much of your team.
- You will be frustrated by people that don't "get it."
- Team members will never make progress.
- You will always have unresolved communication issues.

Whichever your tendency, read this section carefully. In the term Metrics for Assurance, *assurance* means confidence. Assurance means certainty. Assurance means freedom from self-doubt and insecurity.

As you lead change, you will be diving into the unknown—and new future. You will likely face obstacles and opposition. You will *need* Metrics for Assurance.

WHAT GETS MEASURED GETS MANAGED

When my youngest son, Kent, was in college, he ran track for the University of North Carolina at Charlotte. His primary event was the 800-meter race—a brutal half-mile that's a hybrid of distance running and sprinting. It's not for the faint of heart (literally).

In early conversations with his coach, my question was simple, "What does Kent have to do to earn scholarship money?"

Coach Ed's answer was also simple, "Earn points at conference."

So right there in that conversation, we created *pressure*:

- Coach Ed wanted points at conference.
- Dad wanted scholarship money.
- Kent wanted success and to make both of these people happy.

The coach had a very simple way of keeping pressure on Kent: a stopwatch. That stopwatch never lied. It wasn't emotional. It offered no excuse. It simply did its job. It said clearly, "You are running at *this* speed."

We learned that the fourth-place finisher at conference the previous year had finished with a time of 1:52. In Kent's freshman year, his PR had been 1:56. So now he knew: he had *four seconds of pressure*.

At the end of Kent's workouts, the coach wouldn't usually come over and say, "Wow, you really worked hard on that one. Look how much you're sweating. I really think you're getting better!" Nope. The coach simply held up the stopwatch, and Kent read the news.

As long as the coach was measuring Kent's times, everyone knew how to respond. *Are we making progress? Is the training regimen working? Is his time in the weight room productive? Is he eating and sleeping properly?* Adjustments were made to his training routine based on that number, because *what gets measured gets managed.* The metrics provided assurance of that.

This doesn't mean that the coach never praised his efforts; encouragement was important too. But with his goal of shaving four seconds to convert his time to scholarship money, my son needed to be accountable to the numbers. To do so, he needed the transparency of that stopwatch—his Metric for Assurance.

The phrase, "what gets measured gets managed," is often attributed to Peter Drucker. In my research for this book, I couldn't seem to find if he's actually the original source. In fact, there's some discussion as to the validity of this idea in business. So, rather than debate it, I'll give you my take: in the context of Gentle Pressure Relentlessly Applied, metrics are vital for creating the *pressure*. If you don't measure what you want to change, there will be no consistent pressure on your team. So regardless of any pithy business memes out there, you can know this: metrics create visibility in the process improvement, and metrics help you keep unemotional pressure throughout the process of leading change.

MANAGE ACTIVITY, NOT RESULTS

The danger of talking about metrics in the context of managing people is that some leaders can tend to weaponize metrics. Maybe you've worked for that type of manager:

- "Your numbers are down. Get them up!"
- "We're going to have to let you go. Your shoes-to-socks ratio is the worst in your store."
- "Your Net Promoter Scores (NPS) are twenty points behind the other call center operators."

Of course, metrics are crucial to your overall success in leading change. But we call them Metrics for Assurance. Metrics provide transparency into progress and insights, so that you can act on the parts that need adjusting.

When you manage only results and not people, however, you risk losing your effectiveness. You risk harming your culture. You risk alienating the very people you want to influence.

So, what's the trick to getting it right? It comes in the balance. As leaders, we view the metric, and then use that information (in context) to evaluate the *activities* (which are often tied to behaviors) that created the number. Those behaviors can also be quantified, at least to a degree, in that they are observable actions a person engaged in (or not). In other words, we consider the *results*, and then engage in *relationship* with the person who got them. This balance helps us adjust activities—and thus future outcomes.

Consider these examples, where both the results and relationship are engaged. This allows a manager to explore which activities are contributing to the metrics:

- **If the salesperson's numbers are down, let's investigate why.** Does the salesperson understand the product's value proposition? Does the salesperson have rapport-building skills? Does the salesperson show a lack of confidence? Is the salesperson engaging in another behavior that sabotages customer relationships? Identify the activity that contributes to the low metrics results, and take the appropriate action.
- **If the call center operator's Net Promoter Scores are twenty points below their peers, let's look into the contributing factors.** Does he have a strong, confident phone voice? Does he speak too quickly? Does he know how to successfully manage the phone call? Are there distractions at his desk that cause him to be less focused?

The metrics give us transparency, so we are aware of the behavior. We then must manage the activity that contributes to this outcome.

A common (but ineffective) management shortcut is to begin tracking something without fully understanding its contributing factors. The outcome usually becomes a frustrated team and a frustrated manager. The better path is to explore the metric that will measure the *right* activity. Then you can manage, improve, train, and be assured that you are driving the desired results.

Picture this: in order to enjoy the game of golf more, and with the goal of winning your country club's annual tournament, you've decided to improve your skills. In the interest of saving money, you ask *me* to be your coach. (Full disclosure: I don't know why you're asking. I'm not a good golfer, haven't played in twenty years, and have never coached anyone. But stay with me; I'm making a point!)

So, we head out to the practice tee to work on your driver. I observe that you continue to slice each drive into the woods. Each shot is worse than before, and you're growing more and more frustrated. Exasperated, you turn to me and say, "Help! Can you fix this?"

I take a deep breath, then calmly say, "Yes, I see what you're doing. You keep slicing the ball into the woods on the right. That's not good, and you don't want to do that anymore. So, this time, just go ahead and hit it straight. Right down the middle of the fairway."

I'm certain you would look at me in disgust and wonder why you ever thought to have me be your coach. What did I do? I attempted to manage *results*. When you manage using only metric results, without examining the behavior behind those results, you're doing the same thing: engaging in a process that is useless and frustrating to the person you're managing. And yet, we see managers do this every day.

Instead, your golf game would be improved if you had a coach who observed your swing and said, "Your club face is open when you strike the ball. It looks to me like your grill is open when you strike the ball. It looks to me like your grill is the problem. If you'll rotate your grip slightly away from your target, I think you'll see an improvement. Make that change, and try it again." Spoiler alert: the next stroke brings the ball nicely into the center of the fairway! This is what it means to manage *activity* (which often involves *behaviors*).

Remember, as we've explored, *the metrics create the pressure*. Yet when you attempt to use mere metrics to manage, you'll be in the ineffective position of creating the pressure yourself. This harms relationships, further entrenches poor performance, and makes you "the bad cop." As one of my clients said recently, "Let's make the number into the bad guy." When you do that, you as the manager can get on the same side as your team member—in the interest of their development. Now you both can focus on improving the activities that will bring the results into alignment with expectations.

Here's a simple example from a recent client success. Mark and KJ Jimenez from Red Rock Running Company in Las Vegas were concerned about the seeming poor sales of socks in their stores. At the time of our discussion, Mark wasn't certain exactly how bad the situation was, just that it seemed bad. After a little investigation into his point of sale, he found that the ratio of sock-sales to shoe-sales was about 35 percent. Further research showed that the industry average was closer to 50 percent. (The industry sells about half as many socks as running shoes.) Why is this important? Accessorizing shoe purchases with socks increases overall profits.

And some customers will come in just to buy socks if they become loyal to a brand (or store).

Well, Mark and KJ set about to change that. They did *not* broadcast shame and despair to their staff. ("You're terrible at selling socks! Just look at these numbers! Everyone's better that you are! Get these numbers up!") Instead, they began talking systematically with their team about the importance of socks to their customers' running experience (especially in the desert!), as well as the value of sock sales to the company's financial success.

After securing this Agreement on Approach, the owners showed the team their current performance metrics and set a goal for a better outcome. They began teaching the staff a better way to introduce socks to customers earlier in their fitting process. (They call it PAWS; check it out!) Then they reinforced this new approach with practice and demonstration. They created reminders and incentives.

Slowly, selling socks became the new culture and approach in the store. As of this writing, they've experienced a 48.5 percent growth in sock sales, and their ratio is now at 112 percent of all shoe sales. That's a ratio that exceeds the industry by more than 62 percent—and it's growing.

Be like Mark and KJ: manage activities, not mere results. You'll enrich your relationships, develop new skills, and *still achieve the results you're after!*

USING A DASHBOARD APPROACH

In this world of metrics, I've watched so many managers make mistakes. Their errors ultimately create counterproductive results. Mistakes around Metrics for Assurance include:

- Not tracking metrics at all
- Looking at every possible metric
- Using the KPIs to prove a point or intimidate
- Continuing to obsessively review numbers in the interest of perfection

A tendency to overanalyze numbers is why I prefer a "dashboard" approach to metrics use. Your car produces hundreds of thousands of performance metrics in its daily operation. No driver would be well-served by looking at and analyzing this information on a minute-by-minute basis while operating the vehicle. So, modern cars only show the driver what they need to operate the car. In fact, our dashboards have typically come down to offering a simple "check engine" light, which warns us to find an engine expert as soon as possible to diagnose a larger problem. Some of the newer cars today include an app where you can further explore such details as driver habits, mechanical updates, and more. But those are to be viewed after you turn off the engine—not while you're driving! They won't get you down the road in once piece.

Do you remember the Aesop's Fable titled, "The Fox and the Cat"? Here's my paraphrase. One day, the fox and the cat were in the woods discussing their common enemy, the dog.

The fox bragged, "I've got hundreds of ways to get away from the dogs. There's no end to my options."

The cat responded, "Wow, I've only got one trick—but it's a good one."

Just then, they both could hear the sounds of hunting dogs in the distance. Realizing they were getting closer, the cat resorted to its one option: climbing to the top of the nearest tree, safe and secure. And the fox? The fox was torn, limb from limb, while trying to decide which one of his tricks he was going to use.

Making decisions from too much data has its own inherent challenges. People who prefer data-driven decisions can fall into the trap of making sure *all information is considered* before finalizing an approach. This is what Winston Churchill meant when he said, "Perfection is the enemy of progress." So, while I've been urging you to add metrics to your leadership tactics, this is your reminder to do so with perspective. Focus your efforts toward those numbers that make the biggest difference, then act.

Leslie and I were in a meeting with twenty of the country's leading running product retailers several years ago. Matthew Byrne, the cofounder of Brooklyn Running Company, was talking about his approach to decision-making in the fast-paced world of NYC running retail. He said something to the effect of, "We use the 24/70 approach. That is, when we've got an idea that we want to initiate, we get that approach 70 percent of the way planned, and then we implement within 24 hours." That stuck with me. Analysis, data, fact-finding are vital for decision-making. But especially in a change initiative, there comes a time for implementation. Matt's 24/70 concept strikes the right balance.

As you implement Metrics for Assurance in your march toward change, be sure you're not making the mistakes we've explored. The metrics assure and provide transparency. They exist to measure progress, or identify that there is none. The right metrics serve the process and add (Gentle) *Pressure*.

WHO'S THE GOAT?

I'm not a data scientist, but I've certainly experienced a real danger when metrics are involved in business decisions: *confirmation bias*. This is where we go looking for data which supports our own original hypothesis. When this happens, our Metrics for Assurance efforts disappear, and our team will come to distrust us—and the effort.

I've seen many examples of this. Someone who is interested in forwarding a personal agenda argues from the perspective of the algorithm accuracy, rather than focusing on potential business impact. This looks and feels like a distraction—and it is. It's designed to make a preconceived point.

To see this in action, look no further than a group of sports fans using stats to debate which of their heroes is the "GOAT" (Greatest Of All Time).

> **Dan:** "Peyton Manning, QB for the Indianapolis Colts and Denver Broncos, won the NFL's Most Valuable Player Award five times!

No one else even comes close. He's the greatest QB of all time."

Andrew: "Please! Tom Brady, QB for the New England Patriots and Tampa Bay Buccaneers, didn't need MVP awards. He led his teams to ten Super Bowls—winning seven of them. *He's* the greatest of all time."

Dan: "Peyton's all-time pass completion rating is 1.5 percent higher than Tom's. Peyton's the GOAT."

Andrew: "Tom's all-time QB passer rating is 97.2 to Peyton's 96.5. Tom's the greatest."

Dan: "Peyton holds the single-season record for most passing yards: 5,477. Mic drop!"

Andrew: "Tom broke 5,000 yards *twice!*"

Dan: "Yeah, well, Peyton is in the Hall of Fame, and Tom isn't. Peyton's the GOAT."

Andrew: (Shouting!) "TOM'S STILL PLAYING!!"

I'm sure you've been in these debates yourself. It's human nature to go looking for proof in some numbers for what you already believe. It may feel good, but it does nothing to your credibility or efforts to lead change.

Instead, transparency must be your guiding principle (and desired outcome) when using metrics. Take great care that you're looking at the *right* metrics to create pressure—and not, like Andrew, chasing a preconceived opinion. (But, I mean…everyone knows Peyton's the GOAT.)

CHAPTER 7

TRAINING AND COACHING

I STARTED MY company, The Mann Group, in 2003 as a training organization. We train organizations and individuals on sales, management, hiring, strategy, inventory planning, and business leadership (including emotional intelligence).

We even teach people how to teach. Training is where we become *relentless* in our pursuit of our change.

So, if Training and Coaching are so central to my consulting business—and one of the four phases of Gentle Pressure Relentlessly Applied— you might think I would lead with it. Why isn't it the first chapter? Why is it buried in the second half of the book?

Because training doesn't always work.

I've seen it far too many times. An organization will hire us (or others like us) to come into their company and "fix" a problem with training. Their reasons vary, but they follow a similar theme:

- We need to increase our sales numbers; let's train staff how to sell.
- Our inventory levels are unbalanced and aging; let's train buyers how to buy.
- Our managers are ineffective; let's train them how to manage.

Yet achieving such objectives through training doesn't always work to instill the necessary outcome: which are the *skills* necessary to do the job. You see, the phase of Training and Coaching must be delivered—and received—in an environment of accountability. The other elements of Gentle Pressure Relentlessly Applied *must* be present:

- There must be an Agreement on Approach.
- There must be the correct Metrics for Assurance.

- There must be a Culture of Accountability.

Without engaging in these phases as part of your change management process, the Training and Coaching can be offered—but not received or internalized. And yes, I realize that we haven't yet reached the Culture of Accountability phase in this book, but although these phases are introduced sequentially, they ultimately must work in synch.

Of crucial importance is that the student must *want* the Training and Coaching. If this is not the case, both the student and the teacher are wasting time. (And this happens far too frequently.) This is why the Agreement on Approach and Metrics for Assurance phases precede Training and Coaching. These two efforts help to create the *gentle pressure* needed for the student to desire the Training and Coaching, as we've discussed in previous chapters. By aligning your team's Agreement on Approach and showing transparency through your Metrics for Assurance, members will be ready and eager for Training and Coaching.

There is a saying—often attributed to Buddha but actually penned by Mabel Collins—which is appropriate here: "When the student is ready, the master will appear." When people want to learn something, it's amazing how much energy, enthusiasm, and effort can be applied to the learning. But this is true *only* when the student desires to learn.

Even though I'm using two words—*teacher* and *student*, which are typically used to describe a classroom—that's not my focus. Rather, I'm referring to learning and growth that are applied in life and business. This learning—and a desire to be agile, by applying new information—is paramount in a change process.

If you're a leader, a challenge you likely face often is finding a team of people who want to change, learn, and grow. Working with people who are content and show no motivation for personal improvement can be maddening. In fact, this sort of rigidity can actually prevent you from achieving your goals.

It's been my anecdotal experience that only about 10 percent of the folks I've interviewed over the years have shown up with the attitude, motivation, and will to learn and improve. Everyone else requires that I've had to take some responsibility to create the environment for learning that motivates people to do so. Creating the motivating environment for learning—that's the real challenge. But there is hope...

Remember the story of Southwest Flight 1380 from the introduction of this book? What if, shortly after takeoff, the flight attendants made an announcement like this: "Ladies and gentlemen, in one hour, we anticipate a major incident involving one of our engines. This will result in a hull breach, and we're going to lose our internal oxygen while flying at 35,000 feet. Many of you may die when this happens. In a few moments, we'll begin a short class to teach you how to properly deploy your air mask so that you can survive this disaster."

Gulp! How motivated would the passengers have been in that situation? Needless to say, "the student is ready"! It is possible to create motivation for training—with the right context and purpose.

In this chapter, I'll be diving into the details of training and how to maximize it (my entire first book, *ORBiT*, is on this very topic). But as an introduction to this phase, I want to reiterate that the Training and Coaching phase without context, metrics, and accountability has only a limited level of effectiveness. Maximize your training efforts by creating Agreement on Approach, adding Metrics of Assurance, and ensuring a Culture of Accountability. Make sure the student is ready.

THE DIFFERENCE

Why do we say Training *and* Coaching, not Training *or* Coaching? Well, these are two very different tactics—and both are needed in leadership. Let's further explore the definition of each, for purposes of this process.

- **Training:** To teach a particular skill or type of behavior through practice and instruction over a long period of time.
- **Coaching:** Giving special focus to a work-related activity, especially to one person.

In the world of sports, I like this analogy:

- **Training:** Baseball practice is scheduled every day. The team does physical warmups, takes batting practice, does fielding drills, and repetitively perfects

their individual playing skills (throwing, catching, running, fielding).
- **Coaching:** During the game, the first base coach directs the specific activity of the base runner according to the current situation. And the pitching coach walks out to the mound to discuss the current situation directly with the pitcher.

Similarly, these same situations occur daily in your business. For example:

- **Training:** Your group goes through training on how to use the new software system with a lecture, breakout activities, and some hands-on time with the new process.
- **Coaching:** As one of your team members is navigating the screens later in a simulation before go-live, you notice them skipping an important step that would save time and reduce error. You chime in to show them how to improve the process from their current screen.

There is a major flaw in the approach that many executives are taking with training these days. That is, there's a move to outsource the training in many companies. Just google the phrase "outsourced training." You'll see hundreds of articles about the value of outsourcing an organization's training needs. Hundreds (thousands!) of training companies have been formed, each of them with a unique focus and specialty.

Full disclosure—The Mann Group is one such organization. Founded in 2003, we consult and train on multiple topics, as I mentioned in this chapter's opening. So it's not that I don't believe outsourced training can work, but it must be done correctly to be effective. And it's often not.

Why are more and more companies outsourcing their training? All too often, training is relegated to the human resources department of a large company. HR professionals are already charged with the responsibility of acquiring, retaining, protecting, and developing a company's people. In most cases, the reality of employment law requires this sort of priority. Because their priority (or skill set) may be in other areas, HR pros will simply find a resource, hire them, and let them build and develop their company's training.

Here's the danger—in times of financial stress, HR needs can be seen as optional, and that's often where budget cuts are made. "Oh look, here's some extra budget money. We spent $250,000 last year on staff training. Since we outsourced that to a training company, we can just drop that line item from the budget. Voila, we have saved a quarter of a million dollars!"

You may be wondering why I'm challenging this thinking. After all, as I said, this is also how The Mann Group makes its money. Let me be clear: using a training professional to help your company improve its training efforts is a necessary reality. But the approach must be on a long-term solution, not a six-hour workshop held once a year. That's why our company always focuses on a "train-the-trainer" approach—so that long after we're gone, the training can continue internally.

So let me make my major point: when you outsource your training to another entity and have a specialist come in from the outside to present a few hours of content, without follow-up or repetition (which can be costly and time-consuming, if you keep bringing in an outsider), you're removing one of the most important aspects of training and development. You have eliminated *accountability* within your own culture (a Culture of Accountability)!

This fact, again, is why I've called this phase Training *and* Coaching. Training that doesn't have some form of ongoing accountability to skills development is rarely effective. Sure, your $250,000 budget on training may look good to some, but its overall effectiveness is questionable. There must be a better way.

There is: train. *And* coach. It's actually the coaching that ensures the accountability. That's why it can't be left out as you *relentlessly* seek to develop the necessary skills for change! Here's how Training and Coaching play out in tandem:

- **Training:** Teach processes that support the student's efforts on the job.
- **Coaching:** Provide an experienced mentor to help the student apply the process in real time.
- **Training:** Present the philosophy and concepts behind your company vision.
- **Coaching:** In one-on-one sessions, apply those concepts to the day-to-day projects, and show how they affect your efforts.

- **Training:** Identify key skills necessary to the job, and show best practices to identify ways to optimize those skills.
- **Coaching:** Put the student with a coach who will supervise the application of these skills in a simulated practice session.

In my first book, *ORBiT: The Art and Science of Influence*, I thoroughly explain this concept. An aspiring pilot takes classes, studies concepts, watches videos, and must successfully answer questions about this information on a test. But the real learning takes place when the student is put in a simulator to practice flying a plane in a safe environment. An instructor (coach) monitors the performance and offers immediate feedback and review. In this way, the student can apply the material they have learned in a safe environment with a coach nearby to ensure the skills are developed.

Any shortcuts you take in this phase will only extend the time to proficiency. Once again, consider this phase in the overall context of the other three:

1. Agreement on Approach
2. Metrics for Assurance
3. **Training and Coaching**
4. Culture of Accountability

Of the four, Training and Coaching will likely be the area you'll spend the most time. It is the secret to being relentless. The superstars who inspire us with their pursuits and accomplishments are relentless in the development of their skills. If you intend to reach those same heights of greatness in your pursuits, you'll need to reexamine your commitment to Training and Coaching—or perhaps make a new commitment. Just like with any new skill, it could feel awkward at first to train, and then to relentlessly pursue coaching. But this is the behavior that should directly lead to your team's ultimate success.

EXCUSES, EXCUSES

In our work at the Mann Group, we frequently use an assessment to identify individuals' and a team's communication and decision-making preferences. The one we've settled on is the DiSC assessment (DiscProfile.com 2022). While the assessment has sixty-four possible placements, the 30,000-foot view offers four primary quadrants that are represented by the four letters:

1. Drive
2. Influence
3. Steadiness
4. Compliance

People who score highest in *Steadiness* and *Compliance* prefer a more left-brained decision-making style. They are objective, fact-based, realistic, and even somewhat pessimistic. Analysis rules the day.

Influence folks are decidedly right-brained. Subjective, emotional and leaning on gut feel, these leaders have a people-first method for their decisions.

And then there are the Ds: the *Drivers*. Over the years, we've seen entrepreneurs, sales managers, CEOs, and other successful business leaders dominate this category. There are an overwhelming number of Ds in leadership. These folks love talking about vision, the future, and the *why* of business. In fact, they are often so focused on the future, they have very little time for the now.

If you have that Driver mentality, pay attention: you probably loved my chapters on Agreement on Approach. You may have underlined entire sections about the Metrics for Assurance and Culture of Accountability. Of course, you wouldn't have it any other way. These elements let you lead with the urgency you prefer: "Get out of my way; there's a future to achieve!"

Training and Coaching, however, will likely feel sluggish to you. Yet one of the big obstacles to progress could be the lack of skills on your team. The big obstacle to Training and Coaching—for you, if you are a Driver—will be the patience and investment it takes to develop those skills. Just this week, I spoke with a company executive who felt he couldn't spend $10,000 on a training program, because that money was needed to purchase print ads in a local magazine. Not to diminish any power of advertising, but if a company's people aren't adequately reinforced through Training and Coaching, there's a hole that will only grow more gaping. Without the right skills development, your change effort will get sucked into that hole.

Look at these additional excuses for not Training and Coaching:

- "We're just too busy. The phones are ringing, with customers streaming through the door. We can't get to everyone, so it's all-hands-on-deck. Even if things aren't perfect, at least customers are being helped." (This will catch up to you as you grow—or as your competition grows!)
- "There's no way to measure results." (There is; you just have to find it.)
- "Employees find it demeaning to be 'trained.' It makes them uncomfortable." (Then you haven't adequately built engagement in *why* it matters—to the company and to them.)
- "As soon as I invest in their training, employees will leave for another job anyway." (Or they will love you so much, they will stay and lead your division one day when you get promoted!)
- The best training is experience. They'll figure it out. (No, they won't.)

THE LAST PLAYER/COACH

There's a concept that was frequently used decades ago, but it's rarely talked about today: the idea of a *player/coach*. That is, someone who both plays the game (activity) and coaches others at the same time.

Historically, there have been some great ones:

- Bill Russell won two NBA championships as the player/coach of the Boston Celtics.
- Joe Torre actually transitioned from player to coach in 1977. His first year as manager he was also a player for the New York Mets.
- In his last two years with the New York Giants, Tom Landry was a player and assistant coach.
- The last, and most notorious, player/coach was Pete Rose, who held both roles for the Cincinnati Reds in the mid-1980s.

Why did the role of player/coach die? After all, the team could save money by filling both roles with one person. It died because it didn't work. Ultimately, playing and coaching require two different skill sets. Just look at the history of great professional players who failed at coaching: Magic Johnson, Michael Jordan, Isaiah Thomas, Mike Singletary, Wayne Gretzky, and Ted Williams are just a few of the many who were great at playing—not great at coaching.

And then there are people like Mike Krzyzewski, who you probably know simply as Coach K. You are less apt to hear about his playing skills than his legendary coaching outcomes, particularly with the Duke University Blue Devils.

But there are some great examples of leaders who have mastered the player/coach model:

Most conductors demonstrate this concept of player/coach. None come to mind more easily for me than Leonard Bernstein. Throughout his life, he demonstrated extraordinary proficiency playing piano. That led to him to success at Harvard University and the Curtis Institute of Music, as he became increasingly in demand as a performer. His big break came, however, when he stepped in at the last minute to conduct the New York Philharmonic Orchestra on November 14, 1943. He was now both player and coach, and after the success of this night, his life would never be the same (America's Library 2022).

The food network is populated with dozens of examples of player/coaches. That is, there are many chefs who successfully transitioned from someone who could cook, to someone who created recipes, to someone who taught others. The proof of success in their "coaching" came when those they taught could eventually repeat the dish hundreds of times a night. I remember the night thirteen years ago when I went to Emeril Lagasse's restaurant, NOLA, hoping to get a glimpse of my hero in his kitchen. No such luck. His team, however, delivered one of the most memorable dining experiences I would ever enjoy. Player to coach.

The sports industry has produced some strong player/coach examples, at times. As a football fan, I must reference the on-field examples of the two best player/coach examples from the past decade: Tom Brady and Peyton Manning. Watching either of these MVPs play provided a masterclass in being the coach on the field, while simultaneously being the best player on the field.

Let's acknowledge this reality: you can count the successful examples of a player/coach on your fingers. There aren't many of them, because it's so hard to do. Despite its difficulty, you may still have to serve in that role. Your organization may need that from you. If so, beware of some tendencies:

- It's sometimes a lazy (or shortsighted) choice to take the best player and make them the coach.
- If you're a great player who's been pressed into the simultaneous role of coach, you'll likely prefer reverting back to your player role most of the time. (This week, a sales manager told me, "I get frustrated trying to teach new people how to sell, so I just move them out of the way and do it myself!")
- Don't forget that the skill set for a player is different from the skill set of a coach. If you've mastered the role of player and now you're also a coach, you'll need to dedicate an equal amount of time learning how to be a master coach.
- It's also difficult for others to break the habits of player in order to create the new behaviors of coach. Give them time.

Bottom line: If you're in the role of player/coach, do this:

- Dedicate the appropriate time to each role. Plan well.
- Communicate expectations to your team members.
- Give preference to your role as coach. Success at coaching means less time as player.
- Cover your player responsibilities when you have coach responsibilities. Don't get distracted from coaching.

- *Coaching, done well, eventually covers all of your player responsibilities.* Focus there.

When considering all of these examples and the concepts in this chapter, beware of the "Captain Kirk Syndrome." After yet another heroic scene where James T. Kirk has saved the universe, Commodore Paris asks him to return to Star Fleet and become the vice admiral of the Fleet.

Captain Kirk asks, "Vice admirals don't fly do they?"

To which Commodore Paris replies, "No. They don't."

James T. Kirk smiles as he walks away, "No offense, Ma'am, but where's the fun in that?" (Burk et al. 2016).

If your passion and focus lie in the role of player, then enjoy and commit to it. However, if you intend to lead, you'll see the importance and impact of being a coach. It will pay off for your company, for your team, and for you. Either way, dedicate yourself to Training and Coaching, if you want to be relentless in your change initiative.

YOU CAN'T TEACH A PIG TO SING

As you probably realize by now, my life's work has been in training and coaching. I've written about these concepts, delivered speeches about them, and built my company around them. The very reason for this book is to respond to and address this reality: sometimes neither training nor coaching are sufficient to bring about a change. Now why would I say this when I'm touting the importance of the Training and Coaching phase? Because I think it's important to know what Training and Coaching can and can't do for your organization.

Here's a great quote, variously attributed to Judy Sheindlin, Robert Heinlein, and Mark Twain (you decide): "Never try to teach a pig to sing. It doesn't work and it annoys the pig."

I've been in many training events where no learning took place. I've watched numerous companies and clients offer training to their team members, only to have them experience a lack of progress. Why does this happen? If the trainee is earnest and the trainer is competent, why can't we make progress?

Simply stated, there's usually a hole somewhere. More specifically, one of the other three phases of Gentle Pressure Relentlessly Applied is absent from the mix. Maybe the leader failed to ensure that the team had an Agreement on Approach. Or possibly they failed to add Metrics for Assurance. Or, despite the fact that the training session was great, there was no Culture of Accountability (which we will discuss soon). Ultimately the Training and Coaching phase must reside in an overall effort—including the entire Gentle Pressure Relentlessly Applied model—to guarantee progress.

Here's the postscript from my first book, *ORBiT*:

> *It's a rainy, cold day in Boston—early January 2017. I am on a break from training the fabulous staff at Landry's Bicycles. Todd Ouellette has finished reading this book, and he's giving me his thoughts.*

> *"I loved your book, Dan—very practical and right on point. However, I think you are missing one thing."*
>
> Of course, I'm dying to hear his concern.
>
> *"Here's a key point:* **Once you have taught your team how to do something, you have to focus on maintenance. Measurement, follow-up, and consistency are the secrets to long-term success.***"*

This inspirational thought from Todd Ouellette actually inspired the book you're reading right now! He was right, and this point needed to be reinforced. That is, after you've taught someone something, you must then set about to achieve your (and their) long-term success. The Training and Coaching phase—in conjunction with the other phases—is central to this!

The ongoing effort to train new skills and provide coaching for mastery in those skills creates the difference between leading change and accepting mediocrity. If coaching is implemented after training to reinforce the behaviors needed to succeed in the change, you begin to embed the necessary follow-up that Todd was referring to.

But even that combination alone is not enough. You must consider the longevity of your Training and Coaching—as well as how it's tied to each of the other three phases of Gentle Pressure Relentlessly Applied.

Training and Coaching should not be a one-time thing; rather, in those who succeed, it's a process that is repeated and expounded upon. It's a phenomenon rooted in the desire to learn. That learning becomes exponential as commitment to it grows. Look at these examples:

- Bill Gates reads fifty books a year (Financial Post 2021).
- Michael Jordan's work ethic and commitment to continual learning were legendary. He said, "No one will ever work as hard as I work" (Huddleston 2020).
- Henry Ford said, "Anyone who stops learning is old, whether at twenty or eighty. Anyone who keeps learning stays young. The greatest thing in life is to keep your mind young."
- Harland Sanders, Samuel L. Jackson, Ray Kroc, Sam Walton and hundreds of others found their ultimate success late in life, largely because of their tenacity to learn, improve, and develop skills.

In fact, the ultimate predictor of your venture's success may well be your commitment to the maintenance, consistency, development, and ongoing improvement of your skills. Since this is a personal thing—meaning some will show greater curiosity and commitment to learning—we can't force others to change from our Training and Coaching phase alone. But we can influence how effective our efforts are, specifically by ensuring that the Training and Coaching phase doesn't exist in a vacuum. Rather, Training and Coaching should be integrated into the entire Gentle Pressure Relentlessly Applied method. By aligning your Agreement on Approach, Metrics for Assurance, and Culture of Accountability with your Training and Coaching, you can effectively lead team after team through change. You also will foster a passion for learning in your team members, allowing them to emulate the great leaders we just discussed.

How does this look when applied to the other three phases? Throughout your Training and Coaching, to ensure their long-term success, you can:

- **Reinforce the overall plan which team members aligned to during the Agreement on Approach phase.** For example, you can share: "We're learning how to use this new system, so we can commit to our plan of *providing our patients with more access to their healthcare information—minimizing the need for numerous inquiries, while improving patient care.*"
- **Tie your learning outcomes to the Metrics of Assurance you established.** For example, you can share: "Learning how to implement and use this system should help us to *reduce our number of customer complaints by as much as 25 percent.*"
- **Motivate your team members to consider how your Culture of Accountability requires everyone be fully equipped.** For example, you can share: "Since we're committed to *achieving success with this change as a whole organization, losing no team members in the process,* we must remain accountable to each other as we learn the new system."

"ROLL THE TAPE"

During my years of teaching at Meadowview Christian School in Selma, Alabama, one of the great fall traditions was the Friday night football games of the Meadowview Trojans. One of the "chill bump" moments of each game was the playing of the national anthem.

During those same years, one of the great traditions by the NFL's Dallas Cowboys was the national anthem played at each home game by the iconic trumpeter Tommy Loy. He would walk calmly to the center of the field, and in front of tens of thousands of fans, without any sheet music or any back-up accompaniment, he would flawlessly play "The Star-Spangled Banner." He did so for twenty-two years at every home game.

Fortunately, even though we were multiple states away from Texas—in Alabama—Meadowview had a local celebrity who possessed the same skill. Otey "Bubba" Crisman (owner of Otey Crisman Putters and son of the PGA golfer) happened to be a world-class trumpet player. Drawing inspiration from Tommy Loy, Bubba would solemnly walk onto the football field and play the national anthem as a sea of reverent fans stood silently. This added an "America's team" credibility to Meadowview's Friday-night lights.

On the day of the homecoming game in 1980, Bubba came down with the flu. For the first time in recent memory, he wasn't going to be able to perform. I approached the headmaster, Johnny Grace.

"What are we going to do?"

"We have a backup plan for this kind of emergency," Johnny reassured. "I have a cassette tape of a college band playing the national anthem. We'll play it over the loudspeaker system from the press box."

I asked him if I could hear the tape. As he hit play and the sound filled the room, I knew within seconds that it wouldn't be an adequate replacement for our legendary trumpeter. In fact, the sound was awful—with poor audio quality and a complete absence of the dignity of Bubba's version. I couldn't imagine that sound blaring across our stadium speakers to start such an important home game.

But: I. Had. An idea. *I* would play it! I mean, I'd played trumpet in my high school band back in Tarboro, North Carolina. Sure that was ten years ago, but playing trumpet was just like riding a bike, I was sure.

I found the sheet music and went to the choir room to practice. My first attempt was just good enough to convince myself that I'd made the right decision. I could do it!

I went back to Johnny and let him know, "We're on!"

I practiced throughout the day, each time sounding better than the time before. But something happened three hours after my practice sessions began. I hadn't picked up a trumpet in ten years. I didn't have the strength in my lips to maintain the song's high notes (and the national anthem has some high notes!). So I stopped the practice sessions. I felt that I'd regain my strength in time for kickoff, and everything would work out fine.

As the hour drew near, I grew more and more concerned. Would this become an inspiring story of a substitute performance by an *unexpected hero*? That's the image I wanted to invest in. But I had doubt. What if it (and I) became a *historic failure* in front of the hometown fans?

I mitigated my risk: I would play the national anthem from *inside the press box*, not on the field. This way, I could have the music in front of me. And at the last minute, I asked Johnnie to keep the tape of the marching bands version nearby.

The moment arrived. "And now, with our national anthem, one of our teachers, Dan Mann!"

As I put the trumpet to my lips and filled the stadium with sound, the first measures went well.

"O say can you see, by the dawn's early light, what so proudly we hailed at the twilight's last gleaming."

So far so good. Will they write this up in the local paper, I wondered?

"Whose broad stripes and bright stars, through the perilous fight, o'er the ramparts we watched, were so gallantly streaming."

I'm so glad I decided to do this. The fans deserve it!

"And the rocket's red..."

And then it happened. There was no *"glare."* The notes were too high. The tired lips kicked in (or perhaps they kicked out!), and the sound vanished. The melodic tune, the optimism, the grandeur—all of which I'd heard in my head—had all gone. The fans heard only silence in the middle of my delivery of "The Star-Spangled Banner."

So I said the only thing I could at that point, "Roll the tape," and quietly slipped out of the press box.

Yes, at one time years before, I had been a good trumpet player. I'd taken lessons. I'd learned the national anthem—and had played it hundreds of times (with my marching band!).

What I had *not* done was ongoing maintenance. I had not practiced or continued the development of my skills.

Bubba sure made it look simple each Friday night. But you can bet he put in the hours. He kept his lips in shape, he rehearsed the song to keep it fresh in his memory, and he developed the proficiency needed to perform in such an elegant and flawless manner.

I hadn't done any of those things.

So many of us in leadership change think that we can convene a training session, bring in a trainer, and conduct a six-hour workshop (complete with a state-of-the-art PowerPoint) and thereby "train" our team. But that's not how it works. Skills development takes coaching, alignment, measurement, motivation, and yes, repetition. But it's entirely worth investing in this phase as you seek a Culture of Accountability—throughout your change and beyond.

CHAPTER 8

IMPLEMENTING PHASE FOUR— CULTURE OF ACCOUNTABILITY

RESULTS ARE NONNEGOTIABLE. That's the approach you should take with your employees, for all the reasons we've shown so far in this book. But there's another phase which will reinforce such results, and that's creating and maintaining your Culture of Accountability. The other three phases prime the engine for your change, and your Culture of Accountability gives it the full tank of fuel it needs to thrive again and again.

What do I mean by a Culture of Accountability? This is the environment you develop, which encourages and demands the responsibility of your employees to perform their jobs well. In a Culture of Accountability, staff both understand their obligations and that there will be inquiry and analysis—whether via metrics, coaching, or the insight of a leader like yourself. Such a culture ensures that your well-established and business-wide standards are consistently met—producing an outcome of *integrity*, as everyone contributes their part.

A Culture of Accountability communicates to your employees that you *will* follow up. If you ask for something to be done, you will ensure that it happens—even if that means issuing consequences. That knowledge generates a *gentle pressure* to perform. And as we've established, that pressure is crucial.

Fostering accountability instigates responsibility. When you find that employees *have* followed up—creating the desired outcomes—with a Culture of Accountability, you have reason to celebrate. The best leaders know the importance of such recognition. When expectations are clear and your culture is one of integrity to your goals, these celebrations become mainstay.

In the absence of such accountability, it's easy to slack off or ignore entirely the task and approach at hand. In that environment, duty becomes nonexistent. If there's no consequence for poor performance, why try?

In this chapter, I will discuss two management styles: *hope* and *causal*. A Culture of Accountability represents the difference between a causal or hope environment.

- In a *hope* environment, you cross your fingers and hope things go well; you don't follow up, don't measure the results, and don't hold your employees accountable. Anything could happen!
- But in a *causal* environment, you're in control of the situation. You set expectations, define roles, measure the results, respond to slip-ups or failings (or successes!), and create accountability. In a causal environment, there are fewer surprises or snafus, because expectations are set and followed until completion.

Creating a Culture of Accountability is a concept that's often mistaken for micromanaging. After all, employees are adults—they have an assignment and should know to do it, right? Wrong. Assuming your employees are responsible and don't need guidance simply because they're adults makes, as they say, an ass out of everyone. Following up on your employees isn't micromanaging; it's just *managing*. It's your job as a manager to keep an eye on your employees and make sure they're producing the results expected (and agreed upon). In fact, most employees crave accountability. It's what assures them they have a standard to achieve, and that they're doing their job well.

A Culture of Accountability can create the difference between an operation that's exceptional or just average. It's the guarantor of your Agreement on Approach, your Metrics for Assurance, and your Training and Coaching. A Culture of Accountability reinforces that *gentle pressure*, which when *relentlessly applied*, guarantees results. And results are what we're after.

In a Culture of Accountability, you have the integrity and commitment to do what you've said—and ensure that your team members do the same. You'll enjoy leading a team that understands the concept of commitment. You'll have the security of metrics that transparently tell the story of progress. You'll celebrate success as team members develop their skills through relentless training and coaching.

As you focus your efforts on culture, understand that this management approach isn't always easy. But it's highly satisfying, as you watch people develop, grow, and succeed. It works!

CREATING YOUR CULTURE OF ACCOUNTABILITY

Since you're the guardian of the Culture of Accountability, how exactly do you create it? And then, how do you enrich and protect your culture? Let's dive in and discuss several strategies to ensure cultural success.

Elevate the Importance of Hiring, Onboarding, and Retention

Selecting the right team may become the most important component to guarding your culture. If we were discussing culture in the context of a petri dish, you'd know that it contains a culture, and the addition or subtraction of anything measurably changes that culture.

This same principle is true in your hiring of new people. New people change the culture. It's much easier to hire for the cultural fit you want than to spend time trying to fix or eliminate a misfit later. In fact, Tony Hsieh, founder of Zappos and author of *Delivering Happiness*, took this a step further. He explained their process on new hires to *Business Insider*, "They go through a five-week training program and at the end of the five weeks, they can take $2,000 and quit. We want to make sure that employees aren't here just for paychecks and truly believe this is the right place for them" (Feloni 2016). Hsieh pioneered this program, which was also picked up and adapted by many other leading companies (Canales 2020).

So besides paying people to quit, how can you ensure that only the healthy organisms (great employees) enter your petri dish (company)? Look for a track record of commitment. Look for a background that values metrics. Look for people who are hungry to learn. When you find these traits in new employees, you've won half the battle.

In the 1998 NFL draft, the Indianapolis Colts held the first pick. They needed a quarterback. The consensus was down to two choices. Most experts liked Ryan Leaf, an exceptional athlete and Heisman trophy finalist from Washington State University. Other experts preferred University of Tennessee quarterback Peyton Manning (Foss 2014). History tells us the story: the Colts selected Manning. He led them to the Super Bowl twice (winning once) and had a Hall of

Fame career. Ryan Leaf washed out of the league in less than four years. Hiring the right team members is the first step to guarding culture.

Recognize Success

As I've hinted at, achievement-minded people love to be recognized. They also love to set goals and achieve goals. Having the boss see and value the achievement reinforces all the right things. Done well, it reinforces every aspect of your Culture of Accountability. Boston Consulting Group conducted a survey which generated 200,000 responses from 189 countries. They followed up with fifty interviews. One of their objectives was to determine what factors employees felt most directly correlated to their happiness. Out of twenty-six factors, according to an article published on their website, the conclusion was this: "Globally, the most important single job element for all people is appreciation for their work" (Strack et al. 2014). This was ranked above job security, attractive salary, and good relationships with superiors or peers.

Document Your Why

One of the most misused elements of company leadership can be its vision, mission, and values. Have you ever read Enron's mission statement? Would you believe their values were respect, communication, excellence, and *integrity*? That integrity was defined (by them) as: "We work with customers and prospects openly, honestly and sincerely. When we say we will do something, we will do it; when we say we cannot or will not do something, then we won't do it."

That's a great definition for integrity. So why didn't Enron have any, when the chips fell and they got caught for accounting and corporate fraud? When companies publish these philosophies and don't reinforce or live up to them, whatever integrity they thought they had vanishes. Any goodwill Enron may have built at any time was worthless in the end, because their violation was severe enough to erode it all. Which is why it's so important to document and share your values!

Making values come to life will create accountability. So how do you do this? Start with *you*. Tell your team what you believe. What you intend. How you see the world. What you want to do with your company, and why! Then educate them about your company's vision, mission, and values—and discuss how the company can help make their personal *whys* possible. Communicating these intangibles—and living them—makes them real, and helps insulate and fuel your Culture of Accountability.

In summary, A Culture of Accountability is what you will have when you systematically implement the first three steps of Gentle Pressure Relentlessly Applied.

- You have secured the Agreement on Approach with all members of your team.
- You have applied the right Metrics for Assurance in order to ensure performance.
- You've diligently provided Training and Coaching for your team to develop their skills.

Now it is your priority to guard your Culture of Accountability. Sounds simple, right?

FOLLOW UP!

Ed Bachrach was the fourth-generation owner of Bachrach men's clothing. He was my boss for the final years of my work there as VP of retail, where I was responsible for the operation, customer experience, sales, and profitability of our seventy-five stores.

Ed was also the embodiment of Gentle Pressure Relentlessly Applied. Honestly, I didn't always like his pressure. Most of the time, I didn't prefer his predictable relentlessness. But that was what made him great as my boss. Ultimately, much of my approach to leadership came from his humble example.

One day, Ed walked into my office and said something like, "Dan, I just got a call from one of my friends. He was in the Atlanta store. While he was shopping, he walked into our restroom. Dan, he felt compelled to call me and let me know how bad the bathroom looked. He says it wasn't maintained, it's dirty, and it's an embarrassment to the brand."

Ed wasn't about to let it lie at that. He continued, "Do we have a good bathroom maintenance program in place?"

Defensively, I answered, "We sure do, Ed."

He responded, "Well, are we sure that all of the bathrooms in the company stores are up to our standards? Is Atlanta an anomaly?"

I took control, "Ed, I'm sure we're in good shape company-wide. I'll look into the bathroom maintenance practices in Atlanta right away…"

Ed cut me off, "Yes but I want to make sure we're in good shape in *all* stores."

I took a deep breath. I'd already been focused on not showing him the mental "eye roll" I was holding back, while thinking: *A poorly maintained bathroom in Atlanta is not my priority today. We're a $100 million dollar retailer. We've got other priorities.*

But in the interest of making this go away, I said, "I'm going to take care of this today. I'll send out a memo company-wide addressing this very issue."

Ed left, and I called my secretary into my office. I dictated with a vengeance:

> *Bachrach employees, please refer to our company bathroom standards, which are in the company employee manual, and ensure that these standards are being followed in your store's restrooms.*
>
> *—Dan Mann, VP, Retail*

A week later, Ed returned to my office with a concerned look on his face.

"Dan, what sort of progress is there with the bathroom maintenance issue we discussed last week?"

Confidently, I said, "Ed, I took care of that last week. Moments after you left, I issued a company-wide memo that addressed the needed changes. We're good."

"Well..." he hesitated, "I grew increasingly concerned about this, so this past weekend I went to several local stores to see this for myself. I have to tell you, Dan, I was not happy with what I saw. None of the three stores I visited were up to company standards. Now I'm interested in what you're going to do about this. I'm deeply concerned that another of our good customers is going to experience this declining standard in our restrooms."

Standing up (for impact), I said, "Ed, I will take care of this today."

I had my secretary gather an emergency conference call with all regional managers, district managers, and visual managers within the hour.

I began sternly, "Hey folks, listen, I've had Ed Bachrach in my office two times in the past week addressing our poor bathroom maintenance. You may remember that I sent out a memo last week to the entire company, reminding everyone of how important our bathroom appearance standards are. Now, I want that memo read out loud at this week's Saturday-morning sales meeting. Print a copy, and hand out that memo to all attendees."

I hung up the phone without allowing comment. (*That should reinforce my point*, I thought!)

Feeling good about my efforts, I didn't give it another thought…until the following Monday when Ed walked back into my office.

"Dan, I want you to call a meeting for this Friday night at 9:00 p.m. (closing time) at our Decatur store location. I want all regional managers, district managers, and visual managers present. The dress code is business."

Friday night? 9:00? These folks live all over the country. The cost! The inconvenience! Oh well, this must be important. Despite my inner dialogue, I made it happen.

Friday night, we walked in as the store was closing. Chairs were set up, and Ed was at the front of the room. This meeting was probably Ed's version of a modern-day TED Talk. In the first thirty minutes, Ed went into inspiring detail as to why clean restrooms were directly related to our company vision, mission, and values. He spared no detail. Then he opened the session up to Q&A, and a good dialogue ensued.

Meanwhile, I felt myself slinking to the back of the room and looking for a place to hide. *I know where this is heading*, I told myself.

Next, Ed introduced a new program to guarantee that Bachrach men's clothing would have a clean bathroom in every store, every hour of every day. The program included:

- Having new cabinets sent to every store for supplies
- Supplying every necessary tool and supply for every task
- Outlining every task on a laminated checklist

- Providing a schedule to organize every member of the staff into the process

Ed went one step further. The millionaire owner of the business then demonstrated each of the thirteen steps involved in cleaning the restrooms and gave every attendee the opportunity to do it themselves, with his oversight and coaching. The process took five minutes, and clearly it could be completed while wearing a suit. Everyone practiced.

In conclusion to the evening, he instructed every attendee to go back to their districts (the regions covering every store) and conduct a meeting just like this one—to teach every store manager and assistant manager those techniques and this process. Subsequently, each store manager was to conduct the same meeting in their store with their staff. Deadlines were announced, and the follow-up process was initiated.

I learned—the hard way, through Ed—what Gentle Pressure Relentlessly Applied looks like.

I'm recalling this story, which happened twenty-five years ago. I can still feel the impact it had on me. Was Ed behaving inappropriately? Was he malicious? Was he intending to embarrass me? No, he was just following up. He had asked me a question: "Are we sure that all the bathrooms company-wide are up to our standards?" He did some research and found that there were, indeed, some irregularities. In fact, there were enough irregularities that he returned to my office and reinforced his concern, effectively saying: "After doing some research, I'm concerned about what you're going to do about this."

Finally, after seeing no change, he demonstrated to me (and others) the process he wanted installed throughout the stores. This experience was early in my relationship with Ed. When he and I debriefed about this afterward, he told me, "I wanted to make sure you could see what type of approach we need when it comes to the processes in the company." He continued, "In the future, I don't intend to intercede this way, but I wanted to confirm that you understand what it means to install a workable process in the stores."

I did.

As you create a Culture of Accountability in your leadership role, there will likely be times when it will be uncomfortable for you. Walking back into someone's office to follow up on a previous meeting could make them feel embarrassed. Reminding your employees of a commitment they made could elicit an emotional outburst. Sometimes it may seem easier to avoid that conversation.

Creating a Culture of Accountability, however, will require your integrity. You must commit to follow-up. Do what you say you will do, and don't forget the agreements you and your team members make to each other.

If enforcing a Culture of Accountability in this manner hasn't been your way, your first few experiences will feel forced or uncomfortable. That's okay. After the next five or six meetings of setting expectations and following up consistently, this will become the norm for your team. You'll actually be training them on what to expect from you.

This approach is simple, but it requires intention and discipline on your part. So begin with the end in mind, and create this accountability from the start. Following are some guidelines to help in this process:

1. When you want to create a result, be sure you've implemented the first three phases:
   a. You've secured an Agreement on Approach.
   b. You've applied some Metrics for Assurance and shared them with your team.
   c. You've offered them Training and Coaching.
2. Have your meeting one-on-one with each person to whom you're assigning specific work.
3. Clarify the outcomes and approach for that task. Do this by having your team member tell you (not the other way around!) how it will be done.
4. Set a clear day and time for the follow-up, and get agreement on this timeframe.
5. Create a reminder in your calendar to follow up.
6. At the appointed time, conduct the follow-up meeting.

As you're reading this, I bet you think this is extraordinarily simple. You're right. Still, I see the lack of follow-up as one of the major failings in management, sales, and relationships. What causes us *not* to follow up?

- **Fear.** We may be afraid of the possibility of a confrontation. No one likes that.
- **Lack of confidence.** Are you second-guessing yourself, asking, *is this project really that important?*
- **Poor time management.** Perhaps you forgot the deadline and failed to create any reminders.
- **Concern about micromanaging.** You likely don't want to be annoying and become known as "that boss."

I could probably expand this list, but I'll stop here. Whatever your perceived obstacle, failing to follow up will mean failing to lead. This starts with you. It's time to build your new leadership muscles. Make a commitment to yourself to create a Culture of Accountability, wherein you—and your team—make promises to each other, follow up regularly, and keep those promises. Changing a company culture from irresponsibility to accountability will be no small task. This requires vision, determination, a process, and courage.

If you look in a thesaurus for alternatives to "follow up," you'll see a theme: inquire, inspect, investigate. That prefix "in" is quite interesting. It shows up in some other common places: inspire, inject, initiate, etc. In all of these cases, someone is creating the action. Someone is beginning the process. Someone brings force or movement.

That's right, this is where the Gentle Pressure is *Applied*. In a change initiative, this is particularly crucial. The culmination of the entire process is when you apply it. You do so when you follow up on your expectations. The result? A Culture of Accountability.

And since we're usually supervising adults, this should all go swimmingly (eye roll...).

"THEY'RE ADULTS, THEY SHOULD KNOW BETTER!"

If you've ever experienced frustration as a leader, it's probably because someone didn't do what you expected of them. Are any of these thoughts familiar?

- *Why should I have to tell them to do this?*
- *You would think they'd know this already!*
- *Do I have to tell them everything to do?*
- *Why can't these people take responsibility for themselves?*
- *They're adults; they should know better!*

It's easy to grow frustrated with people. Of course it is; they're unpredictable, rarely reliable, and they never do the things you want them to. Welcome to the world of leadership!

Do you know what usually causes this frustration? You. That is, *your unmet expectations.*

When our expectations aren't met, we commonly feel helplessness, then frustration, then worse. We have no control!

What if I told you that you *do* have an option? It's actually the most logical step you should take, and you've heard it said before: set expectations, and get agreement on them. Yes, this is the solution to address and head off your frustration and inner dialogue about *those people who won't do what they should.*

Unfortunately, too many of us are guilty of going through life with a set of unspoken objectives. You have goals, you have intentions, and you have expectations. However, unlike Ed in the last section, you've never taken the time to express them to your team. No one knows what you wanted. No one else is sharing your goals, objectives, or intentions.

We often make assumptions at our peril, like I did in assuming that everyone would read and apply my memo about the unkempt bathrooms. Remember that people come to the table with *their* experience and perspective, not yours. It's like my good friend, Mike Simmons (Bicycle Warehouse of San Diego), says, "Your common sense isn't my common sense."

So you can't take for granted that you and your team see things the same way or somehow magically know what you want. This directly leads to your frustration, anxiety, anger, or helplessness. It could even lead to your burnout—which would be tragic for you and your change initiative.

That's what it looks like from your side of the table.

What's it like for your employees when you don't clarify your expectations and follow up to ensure they are met? Your team members likely see this as you setting them up to fail. If your continual frustration over unmet expectations is expressed regularly, this will destroy morale, break relationships, and possibly sour the entire workplace. The lack of clear expectations from leadership is one of the greatest causes of workplace dissatisfaction today.

I was in a strategic planning meeting with a small business client recently. The owner convened his leadership team of seven managers for the event. This thirty-year-old company had experienced wild growth during the 2020 pandemic, due to the public demand for outdoor recreation (their niche). So, as 2022 started, it was time to create the strategy for the new year. As we began to build our initiatives for the work ahead, the operations manager, Rachel, stood up and began speaking slowly.

"I don't want to offend anyone in the room, but I feel that we have a major communication problem in our company."

I asked for clarification. "Where in the company is the problem?"

She responded immediately. "Right here in this room." She continued, "There is confusion as to who is doing what. There is no accountability for follow-up and no clear process for keeping each of us informed on what the other leaders are doing. Projects are underway with several people that overlap or contradict each other, and no one seems to even know it's happening."

As she paused, Kim, the sales manager, jumped in, "She's right! It seems to me there's a lot of back-channel communication and confusion as to what the major efforts are within this team. As a result, it's hard for me to trust this group."

Rachel concluded, "Ultimately this causes me not to speak up, and keep my opinions to myself. I feel throttled and closed off."

As the room fell silent, I reflected on the results that can come from a lack of clarity:

- Leaders are confused about their contribution and approach.
- A secondary, back-channel communication pattern develops.
- Trust is destroyed.
- Creative leaders are demoralized.
- Managers are uncomfortable contributing, so they hold back.
- Energy is diffused, because there's no organization to the team's individual efforts.
- Frustration abounds.

So, I began to ask some clarifying questions:

- "Where is the company org chart?"
    - Answer: "We don't have one…"
- "When was your last strategic planning meeting?"
    - Answer: "Last year."
- "When are your update meetings on that strategy?"
    - Answer: "We're too busy to have them."
- "Does everyone in the room have a clear job description for the role they're in?"
    - Answer: silence.
- "Logan (owner), is everyone on this team clear about the company's mission?"
    - Answer: "I think they should all know what I want. If not, John (GM) can probably speak for me."

I could see the problem. Even though the company was decades old, this was a new team, and they'd simply been too busy to clarify expectations, communicate them to each other, and get agreement on them. The results became painfully obvious. Fortunately, this meeting and Rachel's courage revealed the issue in enough time to take action and create a reset.

When you feel yourself growing frustrated with your team's poor performance—or better yet, before you get to this phase—do these things:

- Document and discuss your expectations early and often. Take no shortcuts in ensuring that each team member understands and agrees.
- Provide lots of opportunities for dialogue about the work, allow for collaboration, and listen to employees' opinions—even when they disagree with you.
- Be cautious that you're not leaning on a preconceived idea about your staff. Ask yourself: *Am I certain this team member knows my expectation? Have they agreed to it?*

Of course, sometimes a team member is just a poor performer or bad fit for the role. But in a Culture of Accountability, the accountability begins with you. Check your frustration at the door. Prevent your reaction over unmet expectations by setting those expectations and regularly following up.

ELIMINATE ALL HOPE

In our Mann University Management Course, we introduce a concept: there are two overarching management styles based on the concepts I introduced earlier in this chapter—*hope management* and *causal management*.

Hope management is what we see too frequently. These managers hope that they will get results despite a series of failed efforts, followed by blaming their team. These leaders likely engage in the following actions:

- Emails are sent out.
- Notes are taped to a mirror.
- Memos are read.
- Leading by example is offered.

But it's not enough. Unfortunately, this leadership style often results in inconsistent—or absent—results. You can hear its effects in the frustration of the manager:

- "You'd think these folks would know what to do without me telling them."
- "I'd hope they would see me doing the right things and pick up on it."
- "I sent out an email; I hope they respond."
- "I'm hoping this week will be better."

Your unmotivated employees love this type of leadership style. There's no follow-up. There's no accountability. Usually, the leader is doing all the work!

I was speaking with the sales manager of an inside sales team a few years ago. We were preparing for an upcoming training session with her customer service agents. I asked, "Do your agents know the company's vision, mission, and values?"

He answered, "One would *hope* so…" (Insert your own face plant here…)

Hope is a powerful concept in many settings, but it's not sufficient as a management strategy. As we've established, you're in the business of *change management. Hope management*—that is, managing based on the mere hope that people understand and will meet expectations—creates frustration, inconsistency, declining standards, turnover (you'll lose all of your achievement-oriented team members), and little in the way of measurable improvement.

Eliminate hope as a management style.

I didn't misspell that second management style: *causal.* The root word is *cause*, as in, to *cause*. Synonyms for causal are *constructive, productive, consequential, influential, activation, inaugurate.*

The causal leader is focused on results. Those results occur because of the clear process, attention to detail, and follow-up created by the leader.

These two management styles are easy to contrast:

With hope management:

- Expectations are inconsistently communicated.
- Expectations are communicated only in a group setting, without offering feedback.

- Little to no training is offered.
- Few if any resources are given.
- No measurements or KPIs are associated with the project.
- The manager doesn't set a follow-up date/time.
- Passive-aggressive communication is the norm.

With causal management:

- Communication is consistent; the team knows what to expect.
- The manager engaged in lots of one-on-one communication with opportunities for feedback.
- Thorough training is offered, with an emphasis on results.
- A commitment is made to identifying the resources needed, with follow-through.
- A dashboard of the metrics is provided for all involved.
- Clear "mile markers" are given for follow-up, with a reliable review process.
- Clear, direct feedback is provided by the manager.

Now it's time for some self-reflection. Have you been a hope manager in the past? In retrospect, can you see how that approach has produced poor results? Can you clearly embrace this better way? Will causal management virtually assure your success?

Again, we can defer to the story of Ed and the bathroom standards. The approach I used in that story was that of hope management. I gave no specifics in the memo I sent. I didn't offer a reason why. I had no follow-up. And there were no metrics. I just *hoped* that people would get it, and that I'd see the desired results. After all, who doesn't want a clean bathroom?

Conversely, Ed operated from a causal management approach. He systematically followed up with his expectation, creating more and more urgency—and discomfort—for me. He ensured that the team responsible for leading the effort was on board. He provided resources. He outlined and documented a process. He laid out the next steps, with deadlines and accountability. He literally *caused* the result he wanted. That was causal management.

A Culture of Accountability will exist when you, the leader, become consistent with causal management. You see, creating that culture requires constant focus on the goal. It requires attention to detail for the process. It requires that you initiate the action, follow up with your team, and respond to the outcomes, both good and bad.

A Culture of Accountability requires a bit of stubbornness. Most of all, a Culture of Accountability requires real consistency on the leader's part. Your team must come to expect that you will behave the same way when it comes to your expectations. Inconsistency on your part erodes the culture and lessens the results.

Let's see how this plays out with another real-world example…

I was scheduled to conduct a sales training program for Village Bikes in Grand Rapids, Michigan, back in early February 2011. I flew in the night before in preparation for the event. Dale Phelps, the legendary owner of Village Bikes, made arrangements to pick me up from the hotel in time to arrive at his store before the 8:30 a.m. start time.

Overnight, the city received the worst snowstorm of the year, with severe ice and a foot of snow. I awoke to a city covered in white and local news stories of snowplows in ditches and airports shut down. Essentially, the city was closed for business. In fact, when I went down to the lobby looking for coffee, the front desk clerk informed me that the kitchen crew was unable to make it in, and there would be no breakfast served that day. She wasn't sure when their operations would return to normal (she'd been there all night, unable to get home herself).

I called Dale in order to talk through the rescheduling options.

"What do you think, Dale? Should we try this again sometime this spring?"

Dale laughed, "Dan, I'm in my van on the way to your hotel. I'll be there in about fifteen minutes. We're going to have the training today."

I'm a Southern boy and not that comfortable with these road conditions, so I responded in the only reasonable manner, "You're joking, right?"

Dale: "Nope, I've already called all staff. There are six people who can't get out of their houses. You and I will go by and pick them up ourselves."

Sure enough, Dale was there in fifteen minutes. Together we drove out to the countryside, in and out of neighborhoods, and picked up his stranded team.

Dale and his Toyota minivan weren't going to be deterred by a small weather issue. He wasn't hoping to have the event rescheduled. He caused the result he wanted.

The result? We started the training session at 8:15 a.m.—fifteen minutes early! Consider this your case study in causal management.

THE INTEGRITOR

In the late nineties, during my time leading at Bachrach men's clothing, we had a focus on high-quality hiring. We worked with Jerry Bell of the Bell Institute to learn more about the ideal candidate—a person he refers to as an Achiever. In fact, "Achievers" has become the trademarked name of a program produced by the Bell Group to "help you lead like the best in the world with a deep understanding of your personal strengths, weaknesses, and motivations." Inspired by this model and with his help, we developed our own custom language to define our view of the Achiever, the ideal prospect for us to hire.

Bell's premise—which I love—is that an Achiever is someone with an accumulation of six competencies, which are:

1. Creator (creativity used in problem-solving)
2. Survivor (gets up quickly after failure)
3. Producer (gets today's work done today)
4. Team Builder (takes responsibility for the team)
5. Entrepreneur (calculated risk-taker)
6. Integritor (read on for more!)

First of all, let me make sure you are reading the word correctly. I didn't misspell *Integrator*. That's a different word/concept altogether. This competency is Integritor. I actually had to tell my word processor to learn the word. It's not in your dictionary. But it's based on a root word you know (and have heard from me!): integrity. So, to pronounce it, you make your way through the first three syllables of integrity (*in-teg-ri*) and then add "tor" as the last syllable (*In-teg-ri-tor*).

One of the competencies we developed at Bachrach was this last concept: the Integritor. We identified this high-integrity leader as someone who is *courageous, bold, honest, and becoming more so* and *someone who tells the truth and tells it well*. We felt that a person could have all the other competencies, but if they weren't an Integritor, they weren't a fit for our leadership culture.

Since this initiative, I've looked for this trait in subsequent hiring projects, and I've worked on these attributes in my own personal development. I've come to believe this Integritor is my ideal description of a leader.

I often joke about this made-up word, Integritor. "I'd like to introduce you to the next Marvel Universe superhero, INTEGRITOR!" But honestly, the joke isn't far-fetched. This leader is a superhero—capable of effectively leading a team, inspiring their followers, achieving measurable results, and building lasting greatness around a meaningful vision.

If you lead a team and want to supercharge your results and effectiveness, you should seek to become an Integritor. An Integritor is courageous and bold.

So what gives these leaders courage and boldness? I'd say it's less about a personality style and more about their singular focus on an inspiring vision. I've watched as many "leaders" come and go through the workplace, driven only by their personal financial or ambitious motivations. I'm inspired, however, by leaders who are compelled by a clear and challenging vision.

So what's yours? What is it in your life that's worth boldness? What potential future gives you the courage to fight, to sacrifice, to elevate your performance? You'll need to start there if you want to be an Integritor.

An Integritor is honest, and becoming more so. Being honest is probably the most difficult choice one can make. All of us can look back on times when we didn't make the honest choice and can see the pain, aggravation, or disasters it caused. But in the context of leadership, when working with a team, honesty must be the tough choice that you select again and again. That honesty frames our training and coaching, our feedback, and our commitment to measure results.

And of course, honesty is the foundation of a Culture of Accountability. It all begins with your choice to be honest.

Finally—and my favorite—the perfect description of an Integritor is: "tells the truth, and tells it well." Lots of people can tell the truth:

- "You're not very good at math."
- "I don't like this food."
- "You'll never make it as an actor."

- "That dress was a terrible choice."

But how do you tell the truth, *well?* This requires your emotional intelligence. This is where you show a capacity for context. This is where you engage all of your patience, personal awareness, sensitivity, and courage in order to say what needs to be said—but to say it in a way that preserves the relationship.

Years ago (1984), I was speaking to a large group of teenagers and their sponsors in the auditorium of Adrian College in Michigan. It was the final night of a weeklong youth conference. I hadn't prepared well for this speech, and I questioned my approach even down to the final hour before I took the stage.

And it didn't go well. Maybe you've experienced it: 2,000 people are watching you forget your train of thought, or attempt jokes that don't land, or share an emotional story that doesn't make a relevant point. Yes, well, I did all of those things that night. After a tepid response at the conclusion of my speech, I quickly left the stage and made it safely back to the dressing room.

Steve Sigler, a coworker of mine—and an Integritor—tapped on the door and came in. I was embarrassed and speechless. He smiled, putting his hand on my shoulder.

"I know that wasn't your best effort, Dan. I've seen you many times before, and I know what you're capable of. Maybe your preparation wasn't what it should have been. But come out here and look at your audience."

He took me out to see what was happening in the auditorium. No one had left. They were in small groups. People were in earnest discussion about my speech. There was great engagement after all.

Steve said, "Sometimes even our worst efforts can be used for good results. You should feel proud—and do better next time!"

I know that I've been teaching that you should prepare. And I didn't prepare well enough for that speech. I share this story to say that if you don't get it right every time, don't panic, and don't wallow. If your intentions are right, and you realign to the four phases in the book, you can still succeed. Full compliance with this process likely won't come overnight, and that is okay. But commitment to Gentle Pressure Relentlessly Applied will ensure that you are growing in your leadership legacy—and able to lead your organization through the current change, and the next one…

This book has described a process: a process to create change, effectively lead people, and develop a Culture of Accountability in your world. This is the type of leader it takes to implement this process. A true leader is an Integritor. And now you know the leader's secret weapon: Gentle Pressure Relentlessly Applied.

CONCLUSION

WHAT IS IT you want to change? Your team's results? A partner's performance? An employee's attitude? A failing process?

Since you have read this far, you have learned about all the tools you need to lead change. Now what?

Before I send you on your way, let's review the process introduced in this book so that it's top of mind…

Gentle

Your first step will be to look inward to ensure you're emotionally prepared to lead the process of change. Then, remember that any successful change will require engagement of the people you lead, which means you must show respect—allowing others to retain the right to evaluate the changes they're asked to make. To prepare yourself and others, master your listening skills, and create safe environments for the people you want to influence. Remember the attributes of an Integritor: you tell the truth but tell it well. Be Gentle.

Pressure

Anything you want to change must be important to you. If so, make the measurement of it important too. Make the metrics your "bad guy." Your effective use of numbers to measure performance means the pressure is created naturally and without emotion. Here's a fact: without metrics to create transparency to the process, your results can't be assured. Here's another: any numbers you're looking at are likely the result of people's behavior.

Relentlessly

Only if you're clear on why you want change will you be able to maintain the relentless focus needed to see it through. *Unrelenting* literally means to "continue on without fail." This concept speaks to your intention and your focus. Frankly, change is hard. So many leaders lose hope and say, "If no one else is going to care about this, why should I?" Then they go about maintaining the status quo. But since you're still reading, I don't think this describes you! Your change needs a clear "reason why"—pursued relentlessly.

Applied

Here I remind you to initiate the necessary action. If you want change, you must take responsibility—which involves making and keeping commitments. Remember elementary school? Here's what you *didn't* want your teacher to say to your parents, "Dan needs to *apply* himself!" It meant that you needed more action, more focus, more energy in the right direction in order to succeed. The concepts of Gentle, Pressure, and Relentless are straightforward and helpful. Without being *Applied,* your intended change will remain an idea, not reality.

To implement the Gentle Pressure Relentlessly Applied process in your change, follow these phases (and check every box!):

1. **Make certain that you have a full Agreement on Approach.**

    ☐ Double-check your plan. Is it a proven approach? Have you successfully used this approach in the past? Have you learned this approach from a proven resource?

    ☐ Can you explain the rationale for this approach? Is your description compelling?

    ☐ Will this approach make a valuable contribution to the effort at hand? What is the valuable contribution this approach will make to the effort at hand?

    ☐ Have you had this conversation with everyone involved (one on one!)? What was the feedback you received? Was there any pushback, fogging, or resistance?

    ☐ Did you provide others an opportunity for dialogue and ensure they signed on to your approach?

    ☐ Did you shake hands on it?

2. **Create transparency by using Metrics for Assurance.**

    ☐ Are you certain you're measuring the right behaviors?

    ☐ Are the results visible to everyone who's involved in the implementation?

    ☐ Are you guilty of "confirmation bias"?

    ☐ If you can't find a metric to measure, are you sure of the value of your effort?

3. **Focus on Training and Coaching.**

    ☐ Before you begin training, double check that you are successful with phases 1 and 2.

    ☐ Do your trainees want to be trained? What did you do if anyone refused training?

    ☐ Is the training focused on the specific behaviors you want to change?

4. **Create and ensure you have a Culture of Accountability.**

    ☐ Are you regularly following up on all your agreements? How often? Where are you documenting the follow-ups?

    ☐ Are you measuring results and sharing the results (both positive and negative) with the team? How are you sharing? How often?

    ☐ Do you offer consistent training and coaching?

    ☐ Are you taking appropriate action (such as double-checking on the agreement, reviewing metrics, refocusing on training and development, etc.) when someone falls short of their agreements? If yes, then where are you documenting? If no, what gets in the way?

    ☐ Are you having the follow-up conversations even though they may be difficult? If yes, then where are you documenting? If no, what gets in the way?

    ☐ Are there some team members you avoid out of fear of their response? Ask: What is the worst that can happen? Make specific adjustments.

Final Thoughts

It's not easy to initiate change. It's even more difficult to attempt change when leading a team. Here's what *can* happen:

- You can grow frustrated with the team and just do things yourself. While going solo, you'll likely grow more frustrated, passive-aggressive, or sullen. The team may fall into disfunction, and you will still fail to make progress.
- You can become over-controlling and determined to get your result. You may bypass the process and become the "relentless pressure" through threats, arguments, or punishment.
- Out of frustration, you may second-guess the change you want, ultimately deciding it's not worth it and settling for the status quo.
- Failing to accept responsibility, you may blame others in the process and abandon the effort, saying, "It's not my problem." This feels good because if no one else cares, why should you?

If you've been down some of these roads before, you know where they lead: you become uninspired, powerless, and defeated.

This time, choose something different. What is the change you want? What is the great vision that's worth achieving? What is the inspiring effort you'd like to lead? My advice to you is to focus on this *reason why* and then be systematic.

Lead with Gentle Pressure Relentlessly Applied, and create an outcome worth changing for. Then (or as you implement) reach out to me as I'd love to hear your results!

ACKNOWLEDGMENTS

CREATING A BOOK is always a group effort, and in that vein, I'd like to thank the following people and groups.

Leslie, as I stated in the introduction, this book wouldn't exist without your vision, dream, and relentless pressure. You always find the best in me, even if I can't find it myself. Your tireless pursuit of excellence is sometimes intimidating, but always motivating. It's a great life--traveling, working, teaching, playing, creating, and living together. I'm thankful for you every day.

Hank Mann, it's been my greatest joy to see you embrace this work. You are a true model for the value of a family business. Your humility—coupled with your skills at using puns—has been an inspiration. The education industry's dysfunction is the retail world's gain. Your choice to leave middle school teaching created your quote of the year, "I'd like to teach people who want to learn." You've mastered this early in your career, which will become your best advantage (It took me twenty years longer to get to the point where you are today!). I sure love you, man, and I love watching you teach.

Kent Mann, I think your curiosity is what I admire most about you. You always ask the best questions. As I've vetted Gentle Pressure Relentlessly Applied with you and Hank, I've done my best to create a safe environment for your questions and the legitimacy you bring to everything you do.

To Mark and KJ Jimenez: Mark, you and I met after my keynote at The Running Event in 2018. I had just finished my first book but was already talking about this one. Since then, you, KJ, Leslie, and I have gone on quite a journey. You are an educator (an EdD will do that to you….) but you're even more of a student. This book is a testament to you two, who have diligently followed its principles to a T. We've been inspired by you and your ability to make hard choices and implement without any promise of a return (yet your returns have been exceptional!). We relish your success and truly love you both.

Jocelyn Carbonara, I was very lucky the day I found you. After my first book, I knew the value of a trusted advisor for editing. You've been so consistent from day one. You're not likely to get caught up in my short-term enthusiasm (remember the old-fashioned convo?); rather you're singularly focused on the proper result. I need that, and you provide it. This book is dramatically improved because of your guidance. Thank you.

Jenny Lisk, we've never met in person (I hope that changes soon), but I feel a strong kinship with you: Striking out on your own, in the interest of caring for your children. Going your own way regardless of the risk. You are insightful, focused, and curious (that's a compliment!). Thanks for your help now (and in the future!)

George Stevens, you've been great in this process. I've thrown tons of changes your way. You've always responded with, "No big deal, man, here ya go!" You make this look too easy. I expect we'll work together many times in the future. And maybe we'll even get to jam on the guitar a bit too.

To Marathon Sports: The first time I ever presented this Gentle Pressure material in person was at the New Balance HQ in Boston for the Marathon Sports leadership group. That was the start of something great. Colin Peddie, Patrick Gould, and Kevin Dillon were thorough in their follow-up and implementation of the approach. They have validated the approach and offered invaluable feedback throughout. Thank you!

To Bachrach: I spent twelve years at Bachrach Men's Clothing. I came to that company with little business experience. I can safely say that I received a first-class business education during my time there. I like to say that I learned how to run seventy-five small businesses, by supervising seventy-five retail locations across twenty-six states. Thank you, Ed Bachrach, for the opportunity. I don't know that any of us truly appreciated your commitment to continuing education during our time there. We didn't agree on everything at the time, but looking back, I can certify you were right (most of the time!). And I certainly must acknowledge a wonderful friend and mentor from that time, David Van Winkle. David, I find myself quoting you weekly!

To PMI: Years ago, I attended several sessions taught by a group of trainers from Practical Management Inc. These sessions were very informative for me. I have proved those theories time and time again. I'm sure that some of those concepts are included in this book. I think the company has since dissolved, but possibly these concepts live on in the work I've continued in my company since 2003. Thank you!

Hey, Joshua Sprague, you may never read this, but your "Thirty-Day Book Writing Challenge" was the final straw to move me off the stall I was feeling. Following your process while I was camping at the Outer Banks was just what I needed to get this across the finish line. If I ever meet you in person, you'll get a proper thank you.

To the book title team: Deciding the name for this book was quite a journey. At various times, I went through about ten options. After all of that, I went back to my original title: *Leading Change*. My "title brain trust" accompanied me on the journey—voting, offering options, and generally tolerating my indecision. Thanks for all of your help: Todd Dalhausser, Jeff Pressley, Jim and Mandy Leech, Ryan McCarty, Jaryn Pierson, Mark and KJ, Fred Clements, Jenny Lisk, and of course, Jocelyn Carbonara.

CONNECT WITH THE MANN GROUP

Download the Leading Change Checklist
MannGroup.net/checklist

Gentle Pressure Relentlessly Applied is a process that can be systematically followed. Use this free, downloadable checklist to ensure you are following every step as you work toward implementing lasting change in your organization.

Book a Free 30-Minute Business Assessment
MannGroup.net/assessment

Need some help determining where to start? Set up a free, no-obligation call with The Mann Group. Let us help you diagnose where your business is struggling and set a more focused path for the future.

Join the Leading Change Mastermind
MannGroup.net/leading-change-mastermind

This small-group, highly personalized experience is for leaders who want to work individually and together to solve problems while gaining a community that supports lasting business growth.

Take the Leading Change Online Course
MannGroup.net/leading-change-course

"Leading Change: A Culture of Accountability" is an online course that will take you through the philosophy of Gentle Pressure Relentlessly Applied and build your capacity to diagnose your business's challenges and growth opportunities.

Attend a Mann University Course
MannGroup.net/mann-university

Mann U is our flagship training opportunity for leaders who want to implement lasting change in their organizations. These hands-on, in-person events are scheduled throughout the year and are highly experiential in nature.

Bring Dan Mann to Speak at Your Event
MannGroup.net/speaking

Dan has spoken in all fifty states and a half-dozen foreign countries. Why is he so sought after? His speeches offer a unique blend of practicality and entertainment that is sure to inspire your team. Contact us to learn more about bringing in Dan to speak at your company or event.

Hire The Mann Group
MannGroup.net/engagement

Are you ready to create lasting change in your business? Are you looking to solve specific short- or long-term challenges? We help businesses and individuals get unstuck and out of their own way. We will help you plan a better roadmap, inspire your team, and develop a meaningful culture of accountability. Contact us to learn more about how we can help.

ALSO BY DAN MANN

ORBiT

MannGroup.net/orbit

Today, the ability to influence is one of the most marketable skills a manager can possess, and the ability to influence is vital for anyone who wants to accomplish their vision through others. It is especially required for anyone who has a worthwhile cause.

Dan Mann has developed an effective roadmap that increases influence. He calls it ORBiT, an acronym that means Optimized Reality Behavior Training. Here it is in greater detail:

- **Optimized:** To carry out with maximum efficiency
- **Reality:** Real or contrived situations without a script
- **Behavior:** The range of actions by people in relation to their environment
- **Training:** Improving one's capability, capacity, productivity, and performance.

ORBT is a six-step process designed to:

Secure Buy-In	Set Expectations	Increase the urgency needed for change	Create agreement on the approach
Resolve any misunderstanding on how to do something -technique	Teach technique	Develop skills	Increase proficiency

REFERENCES

"Bill Gates Reads Roughly 50 Books per Year | Financial Post." 2021. Financial Post. June 17, 2021. https://financialpost.com/personal-finance/business-essentials/bill-gates-reads-roughly-50-books-per-year-and-remembers-what-he-reads.

Burk, Bryan, Damon Lindelof, Alex Kurtzman, and Roberto Orci. 2016. *Star Trek: Into Darkness*. Film. Directed by J. J. Abrams. United States: Paramount.

Canales, Katie. 2020. "Tony Hsieh, the Late Former CEO of Zappos, Famously Pioneered the Concept of Paying New, Unhappy Employees $2,000 to Quit in Order to Maintain a Happy, Productive Workforce." Business Insider. November 30, 2020. https://www.businessinsider.com/zappos-tony-hsieh-paid-new-workers-to-quit-the-offer-2020-11.

Carbonara, Scott. 2013. *Manager's Guide to Employee Engagement*. New York, NY: McGraw-Hill.

Cohan, Peter. 2021. "A Timeless Lesson of Circuit City's Bankruptcy: Solve the Right Problem." Inc.com. Inc. November 24, 2021. https://www.inc.com/peter-cohan/a-timeless-lesson-of-circuit-citys-bankruptcy-solve-right-problem.html.

Collins, James C. 2001. *Good to Great*. New York, NY: Harper Business.

Covey, Stephen R. 1994. *The Seven Habits of Highly Effective People: Restoring the Character Ethic*. Melbourne: Business Library.

Deci, Edward L., and Richard M. Ryan. 1985. *Intrinsic Motivation and Self-Determination in Human Behavior*. New York, NY: Plenum Press.

Edmondson, Amy. 1999. "Psychological Safety and Learning Behavior in Work Teams." *Administrative Science Quarterly* 44 (2): 350–83. https://doi.org/10.2307/2666999.

Edwards, Roger C., and Walter D. Wintle. 2013. "Thinking." Essay. In *The Little Things and Such: Motivational Poems You Know & Love: Now with Reflection Questions*. Orlando, FL: Edvardson Publishing, LLC.

Eliot, Ray. 2021. "'The Proper State of Mind'." Audible.com. March 24, 2021. https://www.audible.com/pd/THE-PROPER-STATE-OF-MIND-by-Coach-Ray-Eliot-Podcast/B08ZYR62FH.

Ellis, Ian. 1999. "John F. Kennedy - to the Moon." John F. Kennedy - Quote and Its Context - Landing a Man on the Moon - Address (25 May 1961). 1999. https://todayinsci.com/K/Kennedy_John/KennedyJohn-ToTheMoon.htm.

Feloni, Richard. 2016. "Zappos CEO Tony Hsieh Reveals What It Was like Losing 18% of His Employees in a Radical Management Experiment - and Why It Was Worth It." Business Insider. January 28, 2016. https://www.businessinsider.com/tony-hsieh-explains-how-zappos-rebounded-from-employee-exodus-2016-1.

Foss, Mike. 2014. "Peyton Manning Was the No. 1 Pick Because Ryan Leaf Sabotaged the Draft Process." USA Today. Gannett Satellite Information Network. January 21, 2014. https://ftw.usatoday.com/2014/01/how-ryan-leaf-convinced-the-colts-to-draft-peyton-manning.

Gambill, Tony, and Scott Carbonara. 2021. *Getting It Right When It Matters Most: Self-Leadership for Work and Life*. Business Expert Press.

Goleman, Daniel. 2022. "What Is Emotional Intelligence?" Institute for Health and Human Potential. July 19, 2022. https://www.ihhp.com/meaning-of-emotional-intelligence/.

Gutoskey, Ellen. 2022. "How Many Words per Minute Does the Average Person Speak?" Mental Floss. May 22, 2022. https://www.mentalfloss.com/posts/how-many-words-per-minute-do-people-speak.

Herway, Jake. 2020. "Increase Productivity at the Lowest Possible Cost." Gallup.com. Gallup. October 15, 2020. https://www.gallup.com/workplace/321743/increase-productivity-lowest-possible-cost.aspx.

Horsager, David B. 2009. *The Trust Edge: What Top Leaders Have & 8 Pillars to Build It*. Minneapolis, MN: Leaf River Publishing.

Huddleston, Tom. 2020. "How Michael Jordan Became Great: 'Nobody Will Ever Work as Hard as I Work'." CNBC. NBC. April 21, 2020. https://www.cnbc.com/2020/04/21/how-michael-jordan-became-great-nobody-will-ever-work-as-hard.html.

"Item 7: My Opinions Seem to Count." 1999. Gallup.com. Gallup. May 3, 1999. https://www.gallup.com/workplace/237551/item-opinions-seem-count.aspx.

"Leonard Bernstein's Debut." n.d. America's Library. United States Library of Congress. Accessed September 16, 2022. https://www.americaslibrary.gov/aa/bernstein/aa_bernstein_debut_1.html.

Mann, Dan. 2017. *Orbit: The Art and Science of Influence*. The Mann Group.

"Multitasking: Switching Costs." 2006. APA.org. American Psychological Association. March 20, 2006. https://www.apa.org/topics/research/multitasking.

"Re:Work." n.d. Google. Alphabet. Accessed September 16, 2022. https://rework.withgoogle.com/print/guides/5721312655835136/.

Rich Strike's Owner in Complete Shock after Winning Kentucky Derby. 2022. *ESPN.* https://www.espn.com/video/clip/_/id/33876578.

Rich, Mike, and Eric Guggenheim. 2004. *Miracle.* Film. Directed by Gavin O'Connor. United States: Buena Vista.

"Spatial Disorientation Cause of Kennedy Plane Crash." n.d. Logistics Online. Accessed September 16, 2022. https://www.logisticsonline.com/doc/spatial-disorientation-cause-of-kennedy-plane-0001.

Strack, Rainer, Carsten von der Linden, Mike Booker, and Andrea Strohmayr. 2021. "Decoding Global Talent." BCG Global. Boston Consulting Group. January 24, 2021. https://www.bcg.com/publications/2014/people-organization-human-resources-decoding-global-talent.

Welsh, Doreen. 2010. "90 Seconds to Impact!" 90 Seconds To Impact! March 31, 2010. https://90secondstoimpact.wordpress.com/.

"What Is the Disc Assessment?" n.d. Discprofile.com. Accessed September 16, 2022. https://www.discprofile.com/what-is-disc.

ABOUT THE AUTHOR

DAN MANN is the president of The Mann Group, the consulting company he founded in 2003. After writing dozens of training manuals for his clients (Thule, Camelbak, Untuckit, Sun and Ski Sports, Fleet Feet, Canyon Bicycles, Shimano, Brooks Running, Altra Running, CCA Global Partners, and more), he finally decided in 2017 to write his first book, *ORBiT: The Art and Science of Influence*, widely used as a resource for professional managers and trainers everywhere.

His new book, *Leading Change: How to Achieve Superior Results with Gentle Pressure Relentlessly Applied*, was written because his lifelong career leading teams has taught him that there actually is a way to achieve those ever-elusive results you're after. Teaching, training, and leading teams has been his passion since he started his career as a high school teacher in Selma, Alabama. Dan has taught or coached history, art, music, karate, choir, calligraphy, clowning, public speaking, guitar, basketball, and retail sales. In fact, once he develops a passion for a new skill, it seems he sets about to teach it. His highest passion is teaching others *how* to teach.

These days, his other passions include camping (in the twenty-year-old RV that he and Leslie renovated), bourbon collecting, music, smoked meats, bicycling, cooking, fountain pens, and talking about all of these things to anyone who will listen.

Find The Mann Group's podcasts, *Manndatory Listening* and *The Other Side of The Mann*, at MannGroup.net/podcasts or wherever you get your podcasts. Connect with Dan at MannGroup.net.